Science in Geography

2

Data collection

D0681680

General editor:
Brian P. FitzGerald

Science in Geography
2
Data collection

Richard Daugherty

J. J. Aschmann

Oxford University Press 1974

Oxford University Press, Ely House, London W1

Glasgow New York Toronto Melbourne Wellington
Cape Town Ibadan Nairobi Dar es Salaam Lusaka Addis Abab
Delhi Bombay Calcutta Madras Karachi Lahore Dacca
Kuala Lumpur Singapore Hong Kong Tokyo

PRINTED IN GREAT BRITAIN BY OFFSET LITHOGRAPHY BY
BILLING AND SONS LTD., GUILDFORD AND LONDON

Preface

Geography in schools is at present going through a period of change, a change which represents to many a much-needed overhaul, to others an unnecessary dabble in apparently obscure and complicated statistical techniques. Society today is making demands on education which schools and colleges must recognize by taking part in certain changes, if their students are to become adults equipped to play their full part in the society of tomorrow. Much that is still taught is of questionable relevance to the student's needs.

Geography is a discipline which has been slow to carry through at school level the changes that have been taking place in universities. Because of this, ill-defined subject groups, such as environmental studies, social studies, or interdisciplinary studies, are tending to supersede it in schools. Greater co-operation between subjects is admittedly necessary, but one must be aware of the possibility of geography as a school discipline disappearing completely. This would be highly undesirable from an educational point of view, but quite deserved while geography continues to provide little intellectual rigour. The title of a subject, a mode of inquiry, or a field of knowledge is perhaps unimportant, but we do need an intellectually stronger core to what we teach and learn if the essence of geography is not to vanish from schools and colleges.

The changes that *are* beginning to be introduced are making geography more relevant to the needs of students as they become more involved in urban studies and planning, as they begin to analyse the problems of the developing countries, and as they begin to appreciate the problems of resource conservation. These changes are being accepted and becoming established in schools, but there is still very little said about the nature and philosophy of geography on which these changes depend. It is strongly felt that the sixth-form and college student should understand the more important arguments in this field. Only by involving the student in these issues can we justify what is being studied at Advanced Level and beyond.

The literary, descriptive approach to geography, where geography is treated as an arts subject, still has a definite role to play, but a clearer understanding of the nature of geography is achieved with the scientific approach. Such an approach requires the study of spatial patterns and overall systems of operation; it requires a greater degree of precision in measurement and description; it requires some estimate of the significance of inferences and conclusions drawn from the relationships being studied; and above all it requires an attempt to set up generalized theory from which predictions can be made.

The important tests of the success of the approach are:

(1) whether the student has a better understanding of the organization of society in a spatial (geographical) sense; and

(2) whether he has therefore developed a greater ability to make reasoned decisions based on his improved understanding.

On the first point, generalized 'models' or structures of the working of reality (which form the basis of scientific geography) aid understanding and act as pegs upon which to hang further ideas, concepts, and factual material. As far as the second point is concerned, a scientific approach to geography increases the ability to act upon evidence, and, through the development of general theory, allows decisions to be made which are based on a better understanding of reality. Thus courses of action can be better planned, and a more worthwhile contribution to society can be made.

The four books in the Science in Geography series are:

Developments in Geographical Method by Brian P. FitzGerald
Data Collection by Richard Daugherty
Data Description and Presentation by Peter Davis
Data Use and Interpretation by Patrick McCullagh.

The plan for the series came from an idea of Peter Bryan, from Cambridgeshire High School for Boys, whose advice during all the various stages of producing the books has been of great assistance.

Stonyhurst, August 1973   Brian P. FitzGerald

Contents

Chapter 1

General considerations

Introduction

Quality of information

The outcome of any particular inquiry, whether the subject be the world distribution of aluminium production, the pattern of farming in Australia, or the variation in the characteristics of pebbles on Chesil Beach, is dependent on the accuracy, and completeness of the data available. For example, if statistics are obtained for the *volume* of aluminium production by *national* units, and if these statistics refer to some *past* year, the student must look elsewhere for information on which to base conclusions about, say, *current regional* variations in *value* of production within the major producing countries. However sophisticated the techniques he may use to analyse the data obtained, the geographer's interpretation will be dependent on the original information.

Primary and secondary sources of data

An investigator's control of the quality and relevance of data depends on the *scale* of his study, and on the resources available to him. At whatever level a research study is conducted, the quality of analysis will be limited by the nature of the information available. Thus analysis of journey to work patterns in the whole United Kingdom depends first and foremost on the characteristics and availability of statistics gathered in the Census. The researcher is therefore faced with problems such as the lapse of time between the recording and publication of information and, above all, the necessity of operating within the framework of areal units chosen by the Census. On a smaller scale, if the objective is to measure the movement of workers from commuter villages to an urban centre, the student may, by judicious sampling, gather information which is both up-to-date and structured according to his own needs. Any conclusions will of course only apply to the specific cases studied, but their validity in that limited context is much enhanced by the greater control that can be exerted over the original data.

This comparison helps to illustrate a recurring distinction between:
a) **Primary data** obtained by the student in conditions under his control.
b) **Secondary data** derived from sources not under the student's control, and in most cases originally collected for reasons more general than, and often quite distinct from, the objectives of the geographer who later makes use of them.

Whatever the attractions of generating primary data by first-hand investigation in the field, it is essential in solving any particular geographical problem that the most appropriate sources, whether they are primary or secondary, should be tapped.

Original investigation

Much geographical study entails consideration of information both presented and evaluated by others. Consider this statement on the nature of river banks: 'The resistance to erosion will vary with the type of material forming the banks: generally resistance decreases with decreasing grain size up to a certain point, a grain size of 0·2–0·6 mm (Hjulström, 1935), while below that size a considerable increase in resistance takes place.' (Sparks, B.W., *Geomorphology* [Longman, 1960], p. 93). Here a generalization is presented, supporting research evidence is quoted, and, as far as the reader can judge, the information adequately supports the generalization.

However, the geographer who aims at original work must become familiar with the essential techniques of gathering and processing data. This appears in its most obvious form as 'field work'. Frequently the student may learn from the experience of an expert. For example, with guidance from appropriate sources, he may by direct observation be able to understand the significance of, say, Carboniferous Limestone scenery in the Malham area or patterns of land use in the Isle of Purbeck. The more advanced student should, however, also be capable of conducting his own investigation, collecting data relevant to an objective which he has himself defined. He must decide (a) how and where to obtain information, (b) how to prepare material for processing, (c) what methods of analysis to employ, and (d) how to draw conclusions from the processed data. It is the first of these which is the main concern of this particular book, but it must be stressed that the collection of data cannot be completely isolated from the other processes. The student must plan the three subsequent stages before deciding the precise nature of the data he should collect.

The following pages are concerned with the gathering of data from primary or secondary sources in order to carry out a specific investigation. We should note that the assessment of such data involves the same judgements on matters of accuracy and relevance as are necessary to evaluate the quality of information presented in any geographical text.

What is relevant?

You may ask: 'What do we mean by the word "geographical"?' Theories of areal differentiation, regional description, and spatial systems are discussed in S.I.G. 1 (*Science in Geography*, Book 1), Chapters 1 and 3, but whatever the basis of the geographer's approach to his subject, the term 'geographical' used here must be understood to refer to any data needed to solve a geographical problem.

The problem suggested by a pattern of agricultural land use, for example, is indisputably geographical. Analysis may well include the study of other spatial variables (e.g. relief, soil type) which are commonly accepted as geographical. If, however, a survey of farmers' motives in crop selection would contribute to the land use explanation, then such information is equally relevant to the problem. Thus while the geomorphologist considers the physical properties of running water in explaining drainage patterns, the human geographer may include the farmer's motives in his explanation of land use distribution. In other words, the processes at work in producing a spatial pattern may well be non-spatial in character (see S.I.G. 1, Fig. 4.6). The fact that a geographer may be inadequately equipped by his training to explore decision-making behaviour in farming, or the physics of running water, should not blind him to their potential relevance to solving geographical problems.

Examples

No attempt is made in the following pages to deal with all possible sources and methods of collection of all kinds of geographical data. Various examples have been chosen to illustrate the techniques described, providing some general guidelines for any data collection exercise. Examples of aspects of data collection—stating the problem, choosing a sample, methods of field study, locating secondary sources—are referred to in the appropriate chapters. The place of data collection in the overall approach to geographical investigation is illustrated in Chapter 4, where a few studies, representative of the very wide range of possibilities, are described more fully.

Approaching a problem

Aims

Traditionally in geography much stress has been laid on the art of observing the landscape and looking for relationships; for example, the relationship between settlement and river terraces along a major river valley. In the context of an aim such as defining the characteristics or 'personality' of a particular region, the art of observation is an important element in the geographer's battery of techniques. Increasingly, however, as is explained in S.I.G. 1, the emphasis in geography is centering on the analysis, often in statistical terms, of patterns, relationships, and processes in the environment. This **spatial analysis** is tending to supersede **areal differentiation** as the dominant approach to geographical study. 'Measuring variables' has achieved the important status once given to 'sensitivity to landscape', as opinion has shifted on the relative value of different geographical skills. Closely related to this trend is the approach to problems through **scientific method** as outlined in Chapter 1 of S.I.G. 1. Whether the geographer should only adopt techniques which are scientific, in the sense understood by the physicist, is debatable. The definition of a problem for investigation and the methods appropriate to it depend in the widest sense on the individual's view of the aims of geographical study.

Whatever his general approach, in any particular investigation the student must decide: (a) what he is investigating and why; (b) the nature of the results he is hoping to achieve; and (c) the means which he judges most appropriate to that end. It is not sufficient to go into the field with the aim of absorbing the landscape through the 'all-seeing eye' without an understanding of the meaning of 'landscape' and without being aware of the most suitable methods for exploring and expressing its character. Field work textbooks describe complex methods of observing and recording geographical features, apparently assuming that the compendium of knowledge thereby gained constitutes a valid reason for the time spent in the enterprise. It is easy enough to set out with a vague intention of studying a village, a farm or a routeway, to spend a great deal of time collecting information, and finally to return with an accumulation of disjointed, diverse, and often useless pieces of information. These may then be sorted, written up, mapped, and graphed, but the application and interpretation of that information will be difficult **unless its collection was designed with particular aims in mind.** Accurate observation and description are certainly fundamental to the geographer's awareness of the environment, but they are not ends in themselves. They are the means to an end (for example, to the detection of order in geographical patterns and relationships).

Thus a number of questions must be examined before beginning an investigation:

a) What 'hunch' do you have about the problem? Where and in what form is the problem apparent?

b) Which aspects of the problem are to be explored and what results are required?

c) Which methods of observation, collection, and analysis are relevant?

The overall aims and the shorter term objectives of the exercise, clearly stated in this way at the outset, provide the criteria by which the value of collecting any particular piece of information may be assessed.

Defining the problem

Geographers are concerned with the distribution of physical and human features on a stated scale; for example, the pattern of houses in a neighbourhood rather than the pattern of rooms in a house or the pattern of crumbs on the floor. Methods have been evolved and are evolving to study such distributions. Thus most students work in a conventional field of study and with an established range of techniques.

How then do we define the problem in a particular instance? The initial idea or 'hunch' stimulating an investigation may come from one of a variety of sources: an intriguing theory about the zoning of house types in towns seen in an urban geography textbook, observations which seem to contradict textbook theory on drainage networks, a more general interest in an aspect of geography such as road networks, and so on.

Curiosity is often directed towards the pattern of one feature in a particular area. The initial question could be: What is it that determines the pattern of house types in this neighbourhood (or the pattern of stream channels in that drainage basin)? The problem is clearly stated once the area, the terms (for example, what are 'house types'?), and the possible relationships suggested by your 'hunch' are closely defined.

The development of a satisfactory classification of terms might be a first-stage problem that has to be resolved by field study before a worthwhile investigation of patterns can be undertaken. In many instances the investigator has no definite expectation that a particular pattern or relationship will emerge from the plotting of results, but rather a mere suspicion that the distribution will not appear completely haphazard. He may therefore be said to be 'searching reality', looking for some sort of order but without a clear idea in advance of the likely outcome.

Alternatively, an exercise may be planned with a specific result in mind. Rather than seeking some undefined order in a pattern, certain relationships may be expected. To take a simple example, instead of setting out to study changes in the speed of flow along a stream channel, we could anticipate that there is a relationship between increasing speed and distance downstream. Thus, for any particular stream, such a proposition or hypothesis can be tested. We may derive a hypothesis from reading on the subject or from actual observation of a situation. The idea involved need not necessarily be original, nor need we be challenging accepted theory for it to be worth testing. We could 'search reality' recording the pattern of heights of buildings within a town, or alternatively we could set up the hypothesis *that building height decreases with increasing distance from the town centre.* This involves expressing a widely applicable idea about that relationship, then measuring the individual examples in relation to the expected outcome. It may be that the investigation confirms the hypothesis, but it may also indicate some exceptions to the pattern. These can be studied further, perhaps by putting forward an alternative hypothesis, for example *that there is a relationship between suburban office zones and the height of buildings.* We find with this explicit hypothesis-testing approach that not only is the problem clearly stated in advance, but a firm indication of the likely results is given. The follow-up is a matter of interpreting those results by assessing the degree to which the expected and actual outcomes coincide, and finally by accepting or rejecting the original hypothesis. In terms of the initial questions referred to above, hypothesis-testing provides a more limited and rigorous framework for an investigation than the searching of reality.

We can illustrate the stages in proceeding via these alternative strategies in the form of a flow diagram (see Fig. 1.1). Broadly speaking, hypothesis-testing represents the more obviously 'scientific' approach to a problem, structuring an investigation in a series of logical steps. Searching reality, however, may be seen as a prelude to it, in that the tentative generalization which emerges (Fig. 1.1) may be translated into a hypothesis worth testing. Indeed, how else does a worthwhile hypothesis appear, other than by searching reality, either in this formal sense or simply by intelligent observation? The relationship between hypothesis testing and prediction (see S.I.G. 1, pp. 2–3) is shown in Fig. 1.2.

However well organized an exercise may be procedurally, it can only be as good as the hypothesis it tests. If the proposition is of such originality that it throws new light on the subject, then the scientific approach allows it to be adequately tested and developed. For the most part, however, it is

Fig. 1.1 *Approaches to geography*

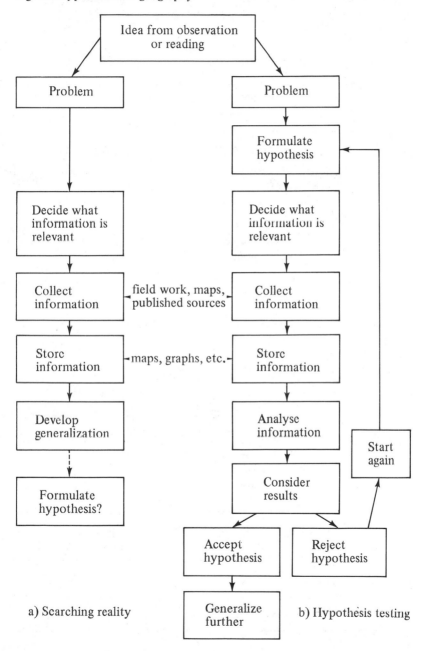

a) Searching reality

b) Hypothesis testing

Fig. 1.2 *The relationship between hypothesis testing, generalization, and prediction in the scientific approach to geography.*

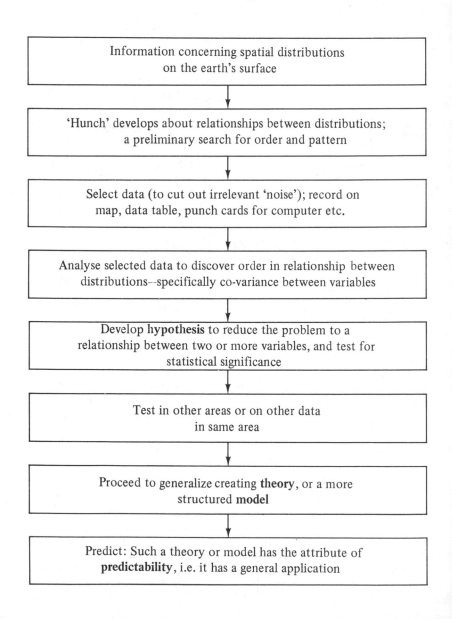

inevitable that we are testing ideas drawn from the main-stream of geographical thinking. To explore a 'hunch' with a view to finding the basis for a new theory of urban structure is self-evidently an exciting and worthwhile enterprise. To test established ideas in a particular context, while less creative in itself, is nevertheless the foundation of a fresh insight to that subject. In conclusion, it should be emphasized that the quality of an investigation does not lie in the label attached to the approach but, first of all, in the clear definition of the problem and, secondly, in the careful design of a procedure for solving it.

Choosing methods

Once the problem has been clarified and the procedure determined, we must decide what information is required and how best we can collect, process, and analyse it. The chapters that follow discuss collection methods and potential sources in detail, while S.I.G.s 3 and 4 review the later stages of an investigation.

At this stage it is useful to consider the relationship between the methods used and the problem. For example, the proposition of the 'rank/size rule' is that there is a relationship between the population size of the towns in an area and the rank or order of those towns in terms of size. When the logarithm of each town's population is plotted on a graph against the logarithm of its ranking by size, a linear relationship can be expected to emerge. Thus in studying the rank and size of towns in any one area, the hypothesis is inseparable from the methods to be used for analysing the relationship between the two variables. Where the idea is less specific, there is a sequence of decisions on methods to be taken. For example, there is no one way of investigating the relationship between two variables such as agricultural land use and surface geology. The variables must first be precisely defined for this purpose, sources of information located, appropriate collecting methods (including sampling procedure) selected, and all this in the light of the method intended to be used to analyse the relationship. These decisions should, as far as possible, be made prior to the investigation since it may well turn out that the analysis to be used will help determine how best to obtain the information.

Whatever the methods chosen, they must be seen as subservient to the problem. Particularly with some of the more elegant methods available for analysing quantitative data, it is easy to allow an attractive method to influence the choice of problem and the way it is studied. Taking a random sample (see p.15) of Dalmatian dogs and measuring the pattern of their spots by nearest neighbour analysis (see S.I.G. 3, Chapter 3) would be using methods much favoured by modern geographers, although the Dalmatian problem in itself may be judged both trivial and obscure! No amount of statistical wizardry in the methods can improve the value of an exercise in which the basic problem is of little importance to the geographer.

Types of approach

Two further examples, followed through in outline from the idea to an organized study, will help to demonstrate the sequence of decisions involved.

(a) Observations in villages might lead up to the hunch that some zoning generally occurs within the pattern made by the age of buildings. If we have no hypothesis on the nature of the zoning, our objectives could be stated in terms of studying several specified villages and plotting the ages of buildings (i.e. searching reality) in an effort to establish some valid generalizations.

(b) Interest may be aroused by the notion that the number of journeys made between two places is partly dependent upon the relative size of those places, and partly also on the distance between them. The 'gravity model' hypothesis (see Fig. 1.3) could be applied in such an instance to predict the amount of traffic moving along routes linking a group of towns. The immediate aim is to test whether the assumptions of the model are borne out in this instance, while the resulting relationship between the observed and the hypothetical patterns will provide the basis for a wider understanding of the forces influencing the volume of traffic movements.

Whether searching reality or testing a hypothesis, once the objectives are clear the methods can be chosen in relation to them. With the village study, the results will be expressed as a pattern of building ages plotted on a map. The plotting could be according to a given classification of building ages, although classification into age groupings could equally well form part of the follow-up if no clearly suitable method of grouping happened to be available. The required information could be obtained from early editions of Ordnance Survey maps as well as from observations in the field. As the aim is not to compile a comprehensive dossier on village buildings, we should not record features such as function, structure, size, or roofing materials. Nevertheless it may be that in the course of this study a hypothesis—perhaps relating age to function—does suggest itself. The development of this idea would then be a 'second stage' exercise, arising out of the first.

Fig. 1.3 *The 'gravity model', derived from physics, provides a theoretical basis for relating by analogy the number of transactions (T_{ij}) between two places (i, j) to the size of those places (usually expressed as population (P_i, P_j)) and the square of the distance between them (d^2)*

$$I_{ij} = G\frac{M_i M_j}{d^2}$$

where: I_{ij} is the gravitational force between bodies i and j

M_i, M_j are the masses of the two bodies

d is the distance separating them

G is the gravitational constant

(a) The gravity model in physics

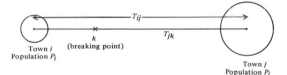

Town i k (breaking point) T_{ij} T_{jk}

Population P_i Town j Population P_j

$$I_{ij} \propto \frac{P_i P_j}{(T_{ij})^\alpha}$$

where: I_{ij} is the expected interaction

P_i, P_j are the populations of the towns i and j

T_{ij} is the time taken between i and j for the means of transport being considered

α is an exponent related to the mobility of the population and may be varied to any value between about 1 and 3 — i.e. it must be approximately 2 in value — to suit conditions in, say Ghana or the U.S.A.

$\propto$ is the sign representing 'is proportional to'

(b) The gravity model in geography, using town populations and time distances

$$T_{jk} \propto \frac{T_{ij}}{1 + \sqrt{(P_i/P_j)}}$$

where: T_{jk} is the 'breaking point' distance from the larger town (j)

(c) The 'breaking point' formula derived from the gravity model

For the **gravity model hypothesis**, the method of analysis is an integral part of the idea, but there are still decisions to be made on the precise nature of the information to be fed into the formula. T_{ij} in Fig. 1.3 could be taken to represent the volume of passenger traffic carried by public service transport between two towns (i and j), related to both the square of the road distance (d^2) between those towns, and to population totals for each town (P_i, P_j) according to the Census. Clearly the selection of the information on which to test the idea of interaction is partly controlled by problems of availability or suitability; the census figure for a town's population may not be considered a realistic index of its size. Such matters must be taken into account in interpreting the degree to which the observed outcome corresponds to the theoretical formula. A second stage investigation could involve studying discrepancies and this might generate further hypotheses to explain them; or perhaps the original hypothesis might have to be amended, for example, by allowing 'd' to represent the time taken to travel from one town to another. Such transformations of distance are more fully examined in Chapter 3 of S.I.G. 1.

Thus the structured solution of a problem may uncover new problems, and the process of defining these problems introduce a new cycle of hypothesis-testing, and decisions.

Chapter 2

Sampling

One of the main problems that we meet in the course of geographical study is that of the so-called 'data explosion'; there are just too many isolated pieces of information concerned with spatial distributions for it to be possible to even start to analyse them all. When we have chosen a particular topic, we may find that a limited proportion of the total elements present will provide us with sufficient detail for study. The technique which we use to choose such a limited body of data is that of **sampling**.

Why sample?

The essence of sampling lies in the fact that a large number of items, individuals, or locations (a statistical **population**) may, within specified limits of statistical probability, be represented by a smaller group of items (a **sample**) selected from the larger group (a **parent population**). It may be that the number of individuals in the parent population, e.g. the pebbles on a beach, is so great that measuring all of them would be impossible from a practical point of view. If we carry out sampling correctly, a limited selection of pebbles will be sufficient for making a generalization about all the pebbles on that beach. In other circumstances, however, measurement of the whole population is possible, but sampling represents a more efficient use of our energy while still allowing us to make reliable statements about the whole population. Public opinion polls announce how a nation intends to vote, or analyse people's attitudes on current issues, but their conclusions are obtained from a sample consisting of a few hundred questionnaires, rather than by consulting everyone in the country. On a larger scale, a sample of approximately 10 per cent of households in the

United Kingdom was taken in 1966 to provide information for the period between the two full Censuses of Population in 1961 and 1971.*

Whatever the level of a study—a university research project or one day spent on a field investigation—the exercise should be tailored so that the objectives can be achieved in the time available. Thus the time allotted to planning, collecting, processing, and analysing should be estimated in advance so that one can reasonably expect to reach some clear conclusion. More and more often, geographers are *measuring* the features studied and recording observations in an accurate numerical form. Such measurement can be a laborious, time-consuming business, and measuring every item may result either in an excessive waste of time on data collection or else may produce a very limited study. Sampling is thus an invaluable way of streamlining the data collection process.

The information needed for a geographical study occurs in a great variety of forms; shops in a town, vehicles moving along a road, slopes along a valley-side, pebbles on a beach, and so on. Sometimes the aim may be to undertake a comprehensive examination of a particular situation. Perhaps we wish to study one village, looking for some patterns within it. In this case, it must be emphasized that any conclusions can only apply to the one village. We cannot assume that any patterns noted are necessarily typical of a wider situation, such as the villages in that area or villages in general. This is in fact a case study, sometimes misleadingly referred to as a sample study   (see S.I.G. 1, Chapter 1, for discussion of the role of case studies). In a sense a case study is a sample, but an uncontrolled one, and therefore any tentative statements which emerge from it about villages in general must be tested in a number of other cases before they can be confirmed as being widely applicable.

The key to success in sampling lies in adopting a procedure which permits us to draw satisfactory conclusions about a parent population from a sample of minimum size.

---

*A summary of the sampling method used in the 1966 Census is given in the introduction to each County Report, and is an interesting example of the complex problems of sampling in practice. It explains there, for instance, how one in every ten *households* was selected and all the residents of each selected household included in the sample. However, with larger establishments such as hotels and hospitals, *every* establishment was included and a sample of one in ten *residents* taken.

Sampling procedure

We must answer several questions in preparing to sample a population:
a) What exactly is the parent population?
b) Which method of sampling is most appropriate?
c) What is the minimum size of sample necessary to give what we could accept as a reliable picture of the parent population?

In some cases the definition of the parent population presents no difficulties, and is simply a statement of what we are studying and in which area. Thus the parent population might be the range of factories in a certain locality, from a list of which a sample could be taken. In other circumstances, however, the very purpose of sampling is to measure, or state the extent of, a large parent population, as with the pebbles on a beach. With a continuous spatial distribution the parent population may be near infinite, as for example the valley cross-sections in one drainage basin. Here, although the parent population cannot be counted, there must be no ambiguity in the stated definition of the population from which the sample is taken. For example, we must decide from what precise area the sample of cross profiles will be taken and by what standard procedure the line of the section will be chosen.

A special case occurs when the subject being sampled involves a **variable time scale**. The beach pebbles and the valley profiles can be seen for practical purposes as samples taken at one point in time. Indeed one aim of our pebble study might be to compare results with another sample taken at some later date. Yet when we try to measure the flow of traffic along a routeway or river water along its channel, the continuous process of change of location through time is central to the topic being studied. What can we say we have sampled if we take a traffic census on a certain road one morning? If we recognize that traffic volume will vary hourly, weekly, seasonally the relationship between sample (our measurements) and parent population (all traffic movements on that road that particular day/week/ season/year) is not readily defined. Thus it is necessary to state not only *what* we are studying (volume and/or type of traffic) and *where* (which road), but also *when* the study was conducted. We must allow for, or concentrate on, periodic variations by sampling at intervals through time.

Sampling methods

Random sampling

Once the parent population has been defined, **each item in that population must have an equal chance of being included in any sample.** Ideally the choice of items for a sample should be **random**, i.e. bias does not affect the process of choice. However, a truly random choice may not always be feasible, and there are some methods of selection designed to speed sampling procedure, which do in fact involve a marginal loss of randomness. The investigator, however, should aim to approach the ideal of random selection as closely as he can. It is easy enough when conducting a questionnaire survey, for example, to question those people who look likely to cooperate. Yet this natural preference introduces an element of bias: 'friendly-looking people' will be over-represented in the sample. In practice such bias might not affect the pattern of results, and the refusal of some people to answer questions will influence the composition of the sample in any case. As a general rule, however, randomness is more likely to be achieved if the pattern governing selection is not that of personal choice but is instead some independent mechanical process such as selection from random number tables.*

Fig. 2.1 *Random number table*

04	67	91	14	11
58	00	73	06	97
14	03	46	16	69
53	56	36	63	81
05	23	59	96	85
72	87	79	85	28
11	43	60	00	53
62	87	24	71	59

Random number tables are so called because there is no bias in the sequence of digits. While the digits may be arranged as in Fig. 2.1, this has no significance, and the numbers may be used singly or in groups, across or down, as required.

Sampling from a list

Let us assume, for example, that the parent population is a list of 200 factories in one area, from which a random sample of 50 is to be taken for detailed study. Each of the factories should be assigned a number from 001 to 200. Then, taking three columns at once and starting from the top left of Fig. 2.1 and working downwards, the factory number 46 (046)

*More complete sets of random number tables are published in, for example, *Cambridge Elementary Statistical Tables.*

would be included, as would the third, number 140, and so on until 50 factories have thus been randomly identified. Irrelevant numbers such as 580 are simply discarded. Further, as in this instance it would be inappropriate to include the same factory in the sample twice, any repetition of a number can be ignored.

We can adapt the procedure so as not to waste time in discarding irrelevant numbers. Each factory in the list could be associated with several numbers, e.g. the first one would be identified when 201, 401, 601, or 801 appeared in the tables as well as when 001 occurred. Thus, rather than discarding the random number 580, it would be taken to identify the 180th factory in the list. In this way, without any loss of randomness, the sample 50 are selected more rapidly.

Point sampling

The same method should be adopted when, instead of items on a list, **the parent population consists of points on a map**, a form in which geographers frequently find their information presented. Rather than assigning a number to each item in a list, we can superimpose a network of coordinates on the map. Thus, for example, the number 046791 refers to a point on the map in Fig. 2.2, the relevant characteristic of which (perhaps geology or altitude, depending on the purpose of the exercise) is then included in the sample. We can then discard irrelevant and repeated numbers in exactly the same way as we did when sampling a list of items. The whole process can be simplified if there is a coordinate grid (such as the National Grid on Ordnance Survey maps) on the map being sampled.

Line sampling and area sampling

Adhering to the same principles of randomness, the patterns on a map could also be estimated by **line sampling** and **area sampling** methods. Instead of seeing the map as consisting of a number of points from which a sample of a given size (referred to as *n*) is selected, we can view the information as an area from which a sample is obtained either by measuring lines across, or by choosing *n* small areas from the total area of the map in question. Coordinates indicated by random numbers are again used to ensure randomness of selection. If, for example, the land use of several farms (i.e. small areas) is to be studied, and the farms are selected from a wider area in which there are many farms, the required number of grid references can be taken from random number tables and used to identify the sample farms, i.e. those within which the random references fall. If the aim is not to study a unit such as a farm but to examine a number of arbitrarily defined small areas, the 1 km grid squares can be used. Thus in Fig. 2.3, random number 5800 indicates the 1 km square of which Easting 58 and Northing 00 form the south-west corner.

There are several methods of obtaining a random line sample, one of which involves assigning values to *each* margin line. This has been done in Fig. 2.4, where, using the tables in Fig. 2.1, 046 locates a point on the southern margin. Continuing down the first three columns of digits in the tables, 580 is irrelevant to this particular area, but 140 marks a point on the western margin. A line joining these two points has thus been indicated by extracting two three-figure combinations from the random number tables. Following the same procedure, the next random line is drawn linking 535 to 052. There is a close connection between studying features along a line drawn across a map, and the well-established field study technique of constructing transects. With a transect, the route across an area is chosen, and selected features are observed and recorded as the route is followed. The transect route, however has probably been chosen with a view to convenient access, and in order to demonstrate particularly notable patterns and relationships. It is therefore a deliberately biased line sample. The traditional transect and the line sample, applied to information gathered in the field or from a map, are essentially similar. The difference between them lies in the randomness of their selection and therefore in the extent to which reliable conclusions about an area, as distinct from impressions, can be drawn.

Once the point, area, or line sample has been built up, conventional methods are used to measure the characteristics of the sample. Thus with a study of agricultural land use, 25 points from a sample of $n = 50$ occurring on grassland would give a result of 50 per cent grassland in the area sampled. Similarly, if half the total length of sample line were recorded as grassland, a 50 per cent grassland result would be indicated; the proportion of each land use type in the area sample could then be measured using squared graph paper.

Point, line, and area methods may often be equally applicable to the sampling of spatial information and the choice of method will then be dictated by circumstances, including the question of the time taken to obtain a satisfactory size of sample. For most purposes, a continuous distribution on a map of such features as altitude, geology, or land use, is most readily sampled by random points. If, however, the aim is to measure drainage density, this might best be achieved by taking the total length of stream channels within a number of randomly sampled small areas. In

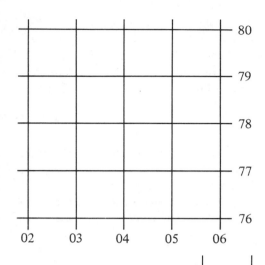

Fig. 2.2 *Point sample*

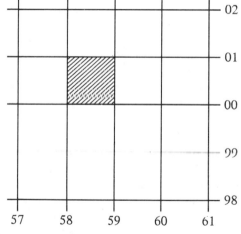

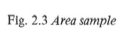

Fig. 2.3 *Area sample*

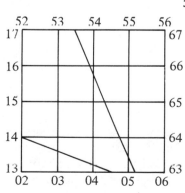

Fig. 2.4 *Line sample*

this case, because of the limited areal extent of the stream channels themselves, a random point sample could give an unrealistic result. If you were
to explore the variations in land use outwards from a city centre, a sample
of random lines radiating from one central point could be used. Consider-
ations of suitability and convenience thus dictate the choice of sampling
methods.

Systematic sampling

There are some short cuts and refinements which can be applied to the
basic methods of random sampling. With a large sample, extracting the
required random numbers and then relating those numbers to the list or
map can be very time-consuming. In such instances a quasi-random or
systematic sample can be used. Rather than choosing each individual
separately, we can use a regular pattern to extract individuals for the
sample. If we study a sample from a list of 200 factories, and choose
every fourth factory on the list, we should reach the target of 50 far more
quickly than by working through random number tables. Similarly, we
can use the existing grid lines for a line sample, and grid line intersections
for a point sample, provided that we always ensure that the whole area we
are studying is evenly covered by those regular patterns. The advantages
in saving of time and effort are clear, but the pitfalls should be equally
obvious. It is possible that the regularity in the sample is parallel to a
regularity in the parent population, so that a significant feature is over-
or under-represented in the sample. A systematic point sample of a planned
landscape, such as the square section pattern of roads across the American
prairies, could conceivably produce a result suggesting that the whole area
is covered in tarmac! Similarly, if the area studied was an American city
designed according to the grid-iron pattern, all sample points could fall on
roads rather than on the blocks between them. These examples illustrate
the general danger involved in using a systematic sample. In most cases,
however, the arbitrary selection of each sample item according to a regular
scheme is just as random as selection by random numbers. Used sensibly,
systematic sampling can often be more convenient than true random
sampling and can be equally effective.

Stratified sampling

Stratified sampling can be used when there are significant groups of
known size within the parent population and it is desirable to make sure
that each sub-group is fairly represented within the total sample. For a
national opinion poll, an ordinary random sample of 2000 *should* give a

fair representation of people by age group, home area, occupation, etc. This can be *assured* by allocating the sample so that each sub-group—young people, factory workers, women—is included in proportion to its known size in relation to the total population. A refinement such as this may be required occasionally, but the basic methods of random and systematic sampling are quite adequate for most purposes.

Size of sample

The decisions on defining parent population and choosing the best sampling method depend to a large extent on commonsense. The problem of choosing the right size of sample, however, is a little more complicated. The simplest rule is that **the larger the size of sample, the more likely it is to give a reliable picture of the parent population.** As a further rough guide, we can say that **the size of n should be at least 30** for satisfactory results to be obtained. Deciding on the sample size in any one case there-fore involves finding the right balance; that is, we minimize the expenditure of time and effort by choosing the smallest sample which allows us to achieve an acceptable and known degree of accuracy. If a margin of ± 10 per cent is acceptable in estimating a feature of the parent population, there is little point in increasing the sample size to achieve a greater degree of accuracy (perhaps ± 5 per cent). The law of diminishing returns also applies so that, although an estimate which is accurate to within ± 5 per cent of the true value can be obtained with quite a small sample, the only way one can be absolutely sure of the true value is by measuring every item in the parent population (i.e. by not using sampling at all).

If a tossed coin is 'fair', there ought to be an equal chance of it falling heads or tails. With a large sample, heads and tails would be expected to appear in roughly equal proportions. With a sample as small as two tosses, however, each of four possible combinations has an equal chance of occur-ring: H–T, T–T, H–H, T–H. Thus there is only a 50 per cent chance of heads and tails appearing equally in a sample of two tosses. Confirmation of the coin's fairness could hardly be gained from such a small sample.

The coin example, where there are only two alternative occurrences, is a special case, and in practice there is usually a large range of possible samples of a given size in a given population. For example, we could take a sample of 50 people from a factory work force of 250 in order to analyse the pattern of journeys to work among the factory's employees. It might possibly happen that the sample consisted of the 50 people with the shortest journeys or the 50 with the greatest distance to travel. Correct use of random or systematic sampling would make this very unlikely, but correct sampling is not a complete insurance against obtaining an unrepresentative sample. Furthermore, because we study only the sample 50, the fact that they are not representative of the 250 would not be apparent. It is therefore important that, with any sample, we are able to indicate the likelihood of an unrepresentative result occurring.

Sampling distribution

The two samples quoted above are the extremes: the first would give a very low value for the average distance travelled to work by those employees, the second a very high value. For any other composition of the 50 sample from the 250 total, the average or mean distance travelled would lie somewhere between those extremes. It is far more likely that the mean of the sample $(\bar{x})$ will lie close to the 'true mean' of the distance travelled by the whole population being sampled $(\bar{X})$. The distribution on a graph of a particular statistic (such as the mean) for all possible samples of a given size, is known as the **sampling distribution**. It is likely, with samples of reasonable size, that the plotting on a graph of all possible sample means of that size will result in a frequency distribution which conforms to the so-called **normal curve**. By referring to the properties of the normal curve (see Fig. 2.5), we can make statements concerning the statistical probability of a certain result occurring when a sample is taken. In practice, those normal curve properties which can be attributed to a sample are used to indicate the measure of reliance. This reliance is stated in terms of the **probability** that the sample value falls no more than a certain distance from the mean of all values in the population.

The **standard deviation*** of the distribution of all possible sample means of a given size $(\sigma\bar{x})$ is known as the **standard error of the mean**. Standard deviation is a very important descriptive statistic, and its calculation and use are fully explained in S.I.G. 3 (Chapter 2) and S.I.G. 4 (Chapter 2). The standard error of the mean approximates to the standard deviation of the population (σ) divided by the square root of the number of items in the

---

*The standard deviation of a population, in this case the population of journeys to work, is found as follows:
  i) Find the mean value of the population $(\bar{x})$
 ii) Find the deviation (d), the amount by which each value varies from $\bar{x}$
iii) Square each deviation (d^2), then sum the squared deviations $(\Sigma d)^2$
 iv) Find the mean of the squared deviations, the **variance** (σ^2)
  v) Find the square root of the variance, the standard deviation (σ)

sample ($\sqrt{n}$):

$$S.E. = \sigma \bar{x} = \frac{\sigma}{\sqrt{n}}$$

One problem, however, is that a vital component in the formula—'σ', the standard deviation of the parent population—cannot be calculated, since the relevant information is unlikely to be available about the parent population. Indeed, the reason for sampling is to estimate the characteristics, as yet unknown, of the parent population. The device of substituting the sample's standard deviation (s) for the parent population's standard deviation (σ) is therefore used. The substitution, though necessary, is obviously not wholly reliable as it is based on the unproven assumption that the sample adequately reflects the parent population.

Fig. 2.5 *Normal probability curve*

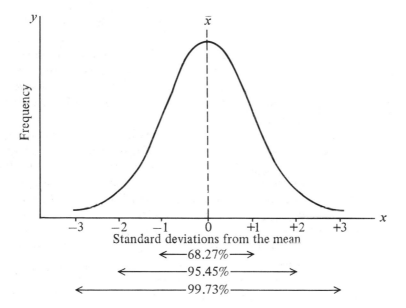

Confidence limits
    Working through the example outlined above will illustrate the several stages of calculation. The mean distance travelled by the 50 employees to

work was found to be 5·3 km, with a standard deviation of 3·7 km. The standard error may be found thus:

$$S.E. = \frac{s}{\sqrt{n}} = \frac{3·7}{\sqrt{50}} = \frac{3·7}{7·1} = 0·52$$

From the normal curve (Fig. 2.5) it can be shown that approximately 68 times out of every 100 the true mean will lie within one S.E. either side of the sample mean. Expressing this in another way, we can say that there is a 68 per cent probability that the mean will lie within the range of 0·52 km either side of the sample mean (i.e. 5·3 ± 0·52, or between 4·78 km and 5·82 km). Similarly, there is a 95 per cent probability of the true mean lying within two standard errors of the sample mean (i.e. 5·3 ± 1·04, or between 4·26 km and 6·34 km), and a 99 per cent probability of the true mean lying within three standard errors (i.e. between 3·74 km and 6·86 km). Stated more simply, there is only a one in a hundred chance that the true mean of the population will lie outside those limits, which are called **confidence limits**. A high degree of probability is achieved only by accepting a relatively wide range of values. In practice, geographers often refer to the 95 per cent probability level when sampling; thus they are accepting the chance that five times out of a hundred the true mean will lie outside the confidence limits defined by two standard errors either side of the sample mean.

Closer study of the standard error will show that any increase in the size of the sample, n, will give a lower value for the S.E. and therefore narrower confidence limits. If the sample had been doubled in size (to 100 in this case), and the same mean of 5·3 km had emerged (in practice it is unlikely that the mean of a different sample would be exactly the same), the standard error would be 0·37 and therefore the 95 per cent confidence limits would be from 4·56 km to 6·04 km. Comparing these limits with those found for a sample of 50 shows that, while they are clearly narrower with the larger sample, the doubling of the sample size has not been accompanied by a halving of the confidence limits.

The standard error of the mean calculation is simpler when the population concerned can be allotted to two categories. Thus a sample could give an estimate that 20 per cent of the land in an area is arable while the remaining 80 per cent falls under other land use categories. Here,

$$S.E. = \sqrt{\frac{p.q}{n}}$$

where p is the proportion in a specified category and $q = 100 - p$. Given a sample of 100 points:

$$S.E. = \sqrt{\frac{20.80}{100}} = \sqrt{\frac{1600}{100}} = \sqrt{16} = 4$$

There is a 95 per cent probability that the true value lies within two standard errors, i.e. that the true percentage of arable land is 20 ± 8 or between 12 per cent and 28 per cent. The confidence limits for each of the other land use categories in the sample can be found in the same way. Whenever sample results are expressed as percentages, this method, rather than the more laborious method described first, can be used.

What conclusions can be drawn concerning size of sample and reliability? The first is that if, as presumably is the case, the sample results are to be a basis for statements about the parent population, then the confidence limits must be calculated and clearly stated. Otherwise the relationship between sample and parent population remains unspecified. Public opinion polls usually say little of their confidence limits (except when, after a wrong prediction in a close election, the 'margin of error' is presented as an explanation). The second, and perhaps disappointing, conclusion is that the confidence limits can only be calculated from the sample data. It is possible, once the sample has been taken from a given population, to work back from the results and estimate the minimum size of sample needed for certain confidence limits at a given probability level. This obviously entails taking a second sample from the same population (for the method see the statistical texts, particularly Gregory, 1968, in the reading list, p. 26). For most exercises, it is sufficient to aim at a moderate size of sample and to accept whatever confidence limits are calculated for the probability level required. **It should be emphasized that it is the size of sample, not the proportion of the parent population which it represents, which affects the confidence limits.** In the journey to work example, the limits for the sample of 50 or 100 would have been exactly the same if the parent population had been 1000 journeys, rather than 250. While commonsense will suggest a larger sample for a larger population, statistical reliability is calculated for the *absolute* value of n.

Further reading for Chapters 1 and 2

A readable and clearly-stated account of sampling methods and the associated problems is contained in:
Reichmann, W.J., *Use and Abuse of Statistics* (Penguin, 1964).

A fuller account of the statistical implications of sampling, also expressed in terms which the non-mathematician can follow, is given in:

Moroney, M.J., *Facts from Figures* (Penguin, 1956).

Two books, the first at a slightly higher level, that discuss the application of sampling to geographical problems, and consider sampling together with techniques of quantitative analysis, are:

Gregory, S., *Statistical Methods and the Geographer* (Longman, 1968).

Theakstone, W.H., and Harrison, C., *The Analysis of Geographical Data* (Heinemann, 1970).

A number of recent geographical publications contain short sections on sampling which give valuable guidance, although not such a full picture as those books mentioned above. These include:

Cole, J.P., and King, C.A.M., *Quantitative Geography* (Wiley, 1968), pp.115–18.

Haggett, P., *Locational Analysis in Human Geography* (Arnold, 1965), pp.191–9.

Toyne, P., and Newby, P.T., *Techniques in Human Geography* (Macmillan, 1971), pp.24–9.

Chapter 3

Collecting information

In theory, once we have defined the subject of our investigation, the next step is to gather the information necessary for testing our hypothesis or for searching a particular aspect of reality. In practice, however, the availability of information and the form in which it occurs may influence the aims and methods of an exercise. In studying the reasons for locating factories in an area, it is often difficult—if not impossible—to obtain useful data and opinions relating to individual factories. Thus it may be necessary to adapt both aims and methods by confining the study to an analysis of the external characteristics of a factory's site and situation. Some familiarity with the range of possible sources of information and with ways of tapping them is essential before any plan of inquiry is finalized. Geography makes use of field observation and measurement, interviews and questionnaires, information published in maps, documents and statistical tables. Any one exercise may well involve a combination of these sources.

Field observation

Any geographer who sets off to do field work is well advised to sharpen his powers of perception in order to observe significant relationships. Elusive features such as erosion surfaces can be noticed only if you examine the terrain so carefully that you can see the several areas of flat land at an approximately uniform height above sea level as the remnants of a once widespread landform feature. Impressions can be recorded in various ways. Field sketching has been developed to a fine art by the geographer concerned to represent in permanent form his visual impression of a landscape. Such observations might also be augmented by a written record and a map of the area.

The strengths and weaknesses of this approach lie in its essentially subjective character. Standing on a hill-top viewing the countryside is an invigorating and satisfying way of obtaining a broad impression of an area. A geographer standing on Wart Hill in Shropshire on a fine day could hardly fail to be intrigued by the Wenlock and Aymestry escarpments stretching away to the east towards the Severn gorge at Ironbridge. From such a vantage point he can draw tentative conclusions about, for example, the relationship between the scarp faces and the distribution of woodland. Using map information he could then measure accurately the degree of association between those two variables. He undertakes this measurement in order to test an idea or hypothesis which emerged from his field observation *that there is a positive correlation between the distribution of steep slopes and of wooded land in the area under study.* This hypothesis can be confirmed or rejected in the light of measured evidence. Many impressions are so trivial or obvious—the relationship between petrol station sites and main roads, for example—that they do not merit full investigation. Field observation will, at first, suggest comparatively few ideas which are important or original enough to be worth pursuing further. Further ideas will be generated by manipulation and analysis of the data originally obtained in the field, or by examination of appropriate secondary sources.

If, as is often the case, a field excursion is undertaken so that we may observe at first hand an interesting pattern of relationships in the physical or human landscape (the existence of which has already been established by others), then providing a record in sketch, map, or note form is clearly a valuable way of consolidating that experience. Where an investigation aims at reaching specific conclusions, first-hand observation of the situation can be vital to developing an idea and directing the general course of the investigation. Once the problem is established, its solution depends on collecting relevant data either in the field or from secondary sources.

Field measurement

Much field measurement involves nothing more complicated than tabulating objects or occurrences. A geographer would not set out to study local weather by recording the changing characteristics in terms of hot/warm/medium/cool/cold or wet/damp/dry. If anemometer readings are not available, he may need to resort to a *qualitative* statement about wind speed by observing the behaviour of smoke, trees, etc. Even then, those observations can be translated into Beaufort's scale of wind strengths from 1 to 12. For example, observation of small trees beginning to sway indicates a wind speed of approximately 33 km/h, registered as Force 5 on the Beaufort Scale. This index is obviously subject to human error of judgement and thus is none too precise, but it does at least give a rough measure which we can compare with other readings at different places and at different times. With an accurate temperature record from a weather station, we can calculate means, deviations, and other statistics in order to summarize the general characteristics of the temperatures experienced at that station. A verbal statement in terms of hot or cool would provide only a subjective record, of little use as a basis for comparison or for suggesting conclusions concerning the processes involved.

In other spheres, steep slopes, large settlements, old buildings, or U-shaped valleys are often described with only minimal reference to their measurable characteristics. Yet the vital questions necessary for real progress are '*How* steep is a steep slope?', and '*What* shape is defined as "U-shaped"?' The excuse that such characteristics are difficult to measure is not an adequate one. Even a relatively crude index of village size, such as that obtained by counting the number of dwellings, is an advance over a purely verbal description. We cannot adequately test a possible relationship—perhaps between woodland and steep slopes or between village size and number of shops—unless both variables are expressed *quantitatively*. Otherwise one person's impression that there is a strong relationship is as unsupported as another's assertion that there is not. There may well be disagreement over how best to measure the variables or interpret the results, but the measurements themselves, as distinct from a verbal description, provide the basis for a valid argument.

Measurements should be as precise and unambiguous as possible. It is self-evident that care must be taken in reading a recording instrument, such as a thermometer, or in counting a number of occurrences, as in a traffic survey. Where observations are to be allotted to categories in a classification, definition of terms is important. When the Second Land Utilisation Survey was initiated, a handbook was published giving information useful for recognizing and classifying the land use types which might be encountered by the thousands of individuals who volunteered to do the field work involved. In this case many observers had to adopt a standardized procedure in order to achieve consistent results, but it is just as necessary to ensure consistency within one exercise. When we meet problems such as the distinction between grassland and rough pasture in a land use study, or the definition of 'break of slope' in a morphometrical map, we must resolve them in the same way each time they occur. Once we have used a certain procedure successfully in one area, we can use the same one to deal with a similar problem in a different area. If a classification of shop types in one suburban service centre has proved workable (see Appendix A pp.56–61), an identical procedure may be used in another centre, thus providing a reliable basis for comparison.

When a classification is designed to meet a specific need, we should carry out a preliminary survey on a limited scale as a check. It is quite likely that unforeseen inconsistencies and omissions will become apparent. Once these flaws have been detected, the classification can be suitably amended. The nature of the classification used is central to the whole investigation, from the collection stage onwards. Thus, whether it is designed for a particular exercise or borrowed from elsewhere, the classification's characteristics—definition of class boundaries, size and number of class units–must suit the needs of the exercise in question.

Once we have decided *what* to measure and the best way of measuring it, we should take care in choosing the maps and constructing the data sheets on which the information is to be recorded. If building characteristics are to be plotted, we will need a map outline of at least scale 1:10 000, and preferably 1:2500, to avoid subsequent confusion in interpreting our work. If we are making a series of measurements, a mistake in recording is less likely if we use a prepared form with appropriate spaces for the details, rather than enter the same data in an ordinary field note-book. Few things are more frustrating than finding, when we are ready to begin analysing the collected data, that a vital figure is illegible or missing. Fig. 3.1 shows a data sheet prepared for recording measurements in an analysis of land use patterns (see p.39).

Questionnaires

If we wish to take measurements on private property, as may well be the case with soil sampling or river flow studies, permission for access will be needed. Where it is evident that the study has been carefully organized, and the approach is polite, most people are willing enough to help. Increasingly, however, as geographers concern themselves more with patterns of social interaction and with the motives governing human decision-making, more than just the *observable* patterns in society must be measured. In these circumstances, in order to study social and economic processes, we need to obtain information directly from members of the public. With a farm study, the geographer has often recognized the value of enlarging on observed information by asking the farmer for such details as livestock numbers and crop yields.

Fig. 3.1 *Data record sheet for agricultural land use analysis*

		Index numbers of survey points							
		1	2	3	4	5	6	7	8 ... n
1. Land use	Arable								
2.	Grassland								
3.	Rough pasture								
4.	Market gardens etc.								
5.	Woodland								
6.	Marsh land								
7. Altitude									
8. Aspect	N.E.								
9.	S.E.								
10.	S.W.								
11.	N.W.								
12.	Nil (i.e. slope<5°)								
13. Slope angle									
14. Soil pH value									
15. Soil water content									
16. Soil texture	sand								
17.	loam								
18.	silt								
19.	clay								
20.	organic								
21. Geology	type A								
22.	type B								
23.	type C								
24.	type D								
25.	type E								
26.	type F								
27. Distance from road									
28. Distance from farm									
29. Distance from town							'		
30. Farm size									

In a different context, the number and kind of shops in a town can be recorded from observation. But it is more difficult to discover the extent of the area served by those shops. If we examine bus services from published timetables we will gain some indication of general movements in the town's hinterland, and by asking shopkeepers for details of the area served by deliveries we will get more information on the problem. However, if we put a series of questions to a sample of the public concerning their shopping journeys, we will have direct evidence of the area served by the town's shops.

These are just two examples of cases where, by questioning the public, we can gain information which helps an investigation in ways that field measurement or secondary sources could not. The difficulties, however, should not be underestimated. People are naturally suspicious of strangers interested in such matters as where they live. Therefore we should explain to the person in question precisely how we intend to use the information. After an initial request for the individual's assistance with the study, we should ask questions which are few in number, briefly-worded, and as unambiguous as possible. Fig. 3.2 is a short questionnaire designed to discover from a sample of the inhabitants of a village the pattern of their movements in relation to urban service centres. The six items/services chosen are broadly representative of different levels of service provision.

Fig. 3.2 *Questionnaire to establish patterns of retail goods and services*

1. Do you live in ....?
2. Where did you *last* buy: a) Bread (if delivery van, state town in which bakery is situated)?
   b) Shoes?
   c) Furniture?
3. Where is your doctor's surgery?
4. Where did you last visit a bank?
5. Where did you last visit a chemist's shop?

It is tempting to include questions which not only ask for information but which also try to discover why people make certain decisions. We might think that by asking direct questions we can most readily learn why a farmer grows the crops he does in the way he does, or why a shopper visits one town rather than another. It must be emphasized, however, that any attempt to analyse people's motives is an extremely difficult and often unproductive course to follow. If, for example, I ask myself why I choose to holiday in Skye rather than to sunbathe on the Costa Brava, the difficulty I have in giving a brief answer to such a question may provide some indication of the problems involved in understanding why other people do the things they do. Furthermore, if we are to analyse a number of replies to such questions we need to construct a relatively objective system of classification for the replies. The farmer's decision to grow barley rather than wheat in a particular field is a very complex one, and he himself is probably not fully aware of all the different factors involved. It would therefore be unrealistic to expect that after a few minutes conversation with a farmer, we should have sufficient understanding of his motives to be able to analyse these objectively (see S.I.G. 1, Chapter 4).

In some instances we can obtain data more effectively by observation than by questioning individuals directly. For example, in studying the extent to which different parts of a town centre are used, we could ask a sample of shoppers which parts they intended visiting. However, it may prove more satisfactory and more objective to take pedestrian counts at selected points to see which parts are the busiest at any one time (see Appendix B).

Residents in an area much frequented by geographers, are likely to become irritable if they are often asked such questions as: 'Where did you last buy bread?' The lesson to be learnt here is not that questionnaire surveys should be avoided, but rather that one should use them sparingly, and in order to collect information not available in other ways, rather than simply to sound out opinions.

Secondary sources

In seeking information for a particular investigation, the geographer should not only be familiar with the methods by which primary data may be generated. A great deal of valuable information is also available in published form. There are, however, two problems associated with the use of such secondary sources: discovering what has been published, and finding out where the relevant volumes can be consulted.

In tackling the first problem, the geographer may, in fact, find that he uses some sources so regularly that he is unaware of their full potential. There is, for instance, a great deal of objective information available in published maps. The publications of the Ordnance Survey, Geological Survey, Soil Survey, and Land Utilisation Survey with their details of spatial patterns, form an invaluable guide for many studies within the British Isles. We should see large-scale maps as *sources* of certain types of information rather than—as is too often the case with O.S. topographical maps—as containing the *solutions* to a remarkably wide range of geo-graphical problems. From an Ordnance Survey 1:25 000 or 1:50 000 (which is replacing 1:63 360) map we can measure the slope characteristics of an area with a fair degree of accuracy, but we should not also expect the same map to provide a full explanation of those characteristics. However, published maps do constitute the most convenient source of quantifiable data, dealing with anything from stream networks to settlement patterns.

There is also much relevant data available in the form of statistical tables, although these are less familiar and more difficult to locate. Standard text-books contain statistical data to a limited extent, dealing with such topics as the mean monthly temperature and precipitation tables (found in every book on climatology) to the statistics of commodity production by value or volume (found commonly in economic geography textbooks). Other general reference books such as *Statesman's Yearbook* and *Whitaker's Almanack* also include some statistical tables, but tables are usually in-cluded as supporting information to illustrate the author's argument. The student undertaking an independent investigation will probably need to refer to a publication where information is tabulated for its own sake (i.e. a data source book).

It is fairly difficult to find source books which are both of sufficiently general application and not too expensive. Philip's *Geographical Digest* is one reasonably-priced publication which presents information, mostly in statistical form, on topics such as population, commodity production, and trade. Revised annually and published in May, it provides useful data, organized by countries, on world economic patterns. By its nature, how-ever, it can only give a generalized picture of these particular aspects of economic geography. Delving more deeply into sources, one runs the risk of becoming submerged in a mass of data published on behalf of govern-ments, national, and international organizations. An attempt to search through the United Nations *Statistical Yearbook* or the *British Census of Population* looking for the required statistics may well dampen the enthusi-asm of even the most devoted and conscientious student. For serious research, a guide such as Harvey's *Sources of Statistics* (Clive Bingley, 1969), is an invaluable aid. It is organized under headings such as popu-lation and trade, and should help in directing you to the most likely source of data.

As a student, you will see little point in using *Sources of Statistics* if the sources identified are not commonly available in reference libraries and would be costly to purchase. This raises the second problem mentioned above, that of locating the required source. Local libraries are likely to prove most helpful in this respect though the number and quality of reference books available will vary from library to library. The final chapter of this book includes some suggestions on sources appropriate to different areas of geographical study. Publications have only been mentioned in this section if there is a reasonable chance of being able to refer to them:

(a) By obtaining the publication from the organization concerned. For example, one would not expect a public library to possess a copy of the Meteorological Office's *Monthly Weather Report* (see p. 45), but a school or college geography department might judge it a pamphlet worth subscribing to.

(b) In a public library. The Library Association has compiled a list of statistical sources which ought to be available on reference shelves in large town and city libraries or at least through loan schemes by which libraries share resources. This recommendation is of course by no means a guarantee that each book mentioned by the Library Association will be available everywhere, but it does give librarians some indication of which sources are most valuable for public reference. Many of the books on this list are mentioned under the systematic headings in Chapter 5.

There are certain collections of statistics which should be on the shelves of any library which has a reference section, even a small branch library. These books, together with brief comments on their possible value to the geographer, are listed here:

Annual Abstract of Statistics (HMSO) includes economic and social statistics for the United Kingdom under such headings as employment, population, fuel, production, distribution, transport.

Monthly Digest of Statistics (HMSO) gives information on the same topics on a monthly basis.

Abstract of Regional Statistics, a relatively recent addition to the list of annual HMSO publications of particular interest to the geographer, provides a regional breakdown, where it is available, of statistics on topics similar to those included in the *Annual Abstract.*

Digest of Scottish Statistics (biannual), *Digest of Statistics for Northern Ireland* (biannual), *Digest of Welsh Statistics* (annual), are all HMSO publications broadly similar in character to those above.

Trade and Industry (HMSO), incorporating the *Board of Trade Journal,* is a booklet produced weekly providing a regular supply of newly published statistics on a variety of subjects.

Where some historical perspective is called for, the *Abstract of British Historical Statistics* (Mitchell and Deane, C.U.P., 1962) has tables on population, agriculture, coal, metals, textiles, transport, trade, etc., with an introduction and bibliography to each section.

The most comprehensive and reliable source of international statistics on a wide range of subjects is the *United Nations Statistical Yearbook* (published by HMSO for the U.N. Statistical Office).

It should be noted that these books, as do many of the sources listed in Chapter 5, arrange statistics by national, or at best large regional, units. Where this suits the scale of the topic under investigation, such an arrangement is satisfactory enough. However, there may well be an unfortunate gap between the information obtained by field investigation and that published in official sources. This is partly because there is a need to protect the confidentiality of the industrialist, farmer, or householder who provides information, and so the information, when published, normally refers to relatively large areas. Details of a farmer's income or a householder's occupation should not, even if it were organizationally possible, be made generally available. The Census of Population, presenting figures by administrative areas and even by wards in some cases, gives details to an exceptional degree. It is in this situation, where published sources are unsatisfactory, that you may be able to unearth data by questioning individuals and local organizations.

You may be able to discover the employment statistics for a limited area from a sympathetic local employment officer. Departments of local administration such as housing or planning may prove co-operative and provide unpublished data. Indeed, some statistics, such as rateable value of property (which may be required for studying a town centre) are usually available for public inspection by arrangement. Whenever it seems appropriate to obtain data at a scale intermediate between published tables and that which the student can reasonably gather for himself, care should be taken in the same way as when conducting a questionnaire survey (see pp.30–33).

Chapter 4

Some examples

There are many problems which can be studied geographically. In any one case the emphasis may be on the patterns in the environment or on the processes at work. Such patterns and processes may be evident at all levels, from the local to the global, and may be seen to belong to any one of the several fields of geography, both human and physical. When we undertake an exercise, our aim should be to throw more light on the problem, rather than to put forward an all-embracing 'solution'. In all probability a worthwhile exercise will raise more problems than it solves, as related issues and influences become apparent.

In general, the more limited a project, in both scale and aim, the greater the likelihood that it will be tackled effectively. This means that the study of a specific aspect of the local environment is more manageable than an attempt to review a world-scale problem. By asking a question such as 'Why is this suburb expanding in the way it is?', we may well be able to test our case study against previously developed ideas. With a global problem such as 'Why is urbanization taking place so rapidly in many developing countries?', information must be gathered from published statistics and research evidence quoted. In a limited investigation, it is difficult to do more than summarize established opinions on the nature of the complex processes involved, so that the small-scale study, by providing *some* new information, is more valuable. In order to illustrate the overall approach to geographical problems, a few examples are described more fully in this chapter. In each case, the aims of the exercise, the information required, and the sampling method are specified. The analysis of results is summarized and possibilities of adapting the exercise, taking it further, or using similar methods to deal with other problems are discussed. (Sources of information for different fields of geography are briefly reviewed in Chapter 5).

Before dealing with any problem, it is important to realize that, as studied, it is only a small part of a larger whole. Each problem must be taken in the context of attempting to achieve a better understanding of reality. In each of the five examples outlined there is, to a lesser or greater extent, an attempt to isolate spatial variables and to relate them in pairs in the form of hypotheses to be tested. This scientific approach is illustrated in Fig. 1.2.

Problem 1
How does the composition of pebble material vary along a beach?

Aim

The aim is to study the relationship between the geological character of beach material and adjacent cliffs on a specific length of shoreline. We can formulate the hypothesis *that the composition of pebbles is directly related to the character of cliff material.*

Method

We can take a sample of pebbles at regular intervals (i.e. a systematic sample) along the study beach, at a consistent position in relation to the water line and the cliff, perhaps just above the high-water mark. We must decide on the points at which samples are to be taken, and then take a random sample of pebbles at each. True randomness is difficult to ensure in such circumstances, but we can come close to the ideal by arbitrarily picking up, say, 20 pebbles in the immediate vicinity of each sample point. Another method is to place a small frame or quadrat at each sample point and include only the pebbles from within that square. For this purpose, four sticks tied together forming a 25 cm square would be quite adequate.

We can then study the composition of the pebbles from each sample point. All that is immediately required is to distinguish between locally derived material and the rest. We may then note the proportion of 'local' pebbles at each sample point and it may be that we find that there is a consistently high proportion of local material all along the beach, i.e. the hypothesis is confirmed.

Implications

Other problems will undoubtedly emerge. Where does the non-local material come from? Why should 90 per cent of pebbles at point A be local while at point F only 50 per cent are local? Is there a recognizable 'longshore drift' of material in one direction? Is there a different pattern of variation when the sample is taken at a location other than the beach surface just above high water mark? Is size of pebble significant? Rather than analysing the pattern still more fully and trying to deduce the processes at work, it is possible—though more difficult—to study processes directly using marked pebbles.

In this case the composition of pebbles in a *coastal* situation was being studied, but we could use similar methods to study the variations in the size and shape of *river-bed* material along a stream's course, or across its channel at a meander.

Problem 2

How far is the distribution of agricultural land use related to the distribution of other variables, such as geology, soil type, altitude?

Aim

The aim, in this case, is to measure the distribution of several variables (such as land use) over a limited area and to assess the statistical correlation between these and each of a set of other variables. One of the hypotheses we can test is *that there is a significant relationship between the type of agricultural land use and altitude.*

Method

An area is chosen and *n* random points located on the map. We then have to visit each of these points to record the relevant characteristics. If we are to analyse the relationship between land use and a large number of variables we have to take a full record of the characteristics of each point as on the data sheet in Fig. 3.1. The exercise is equally valid if land use and only one other variable are considered. Furthermore, where the Second Land Utilisation Survey 1:25 000 sheets are published, we may obtain the necessary information on several relevant variables, including altitude and geology, entirely from maps. Instead of testing the hypothesis using land use information collected in the field, we can test the same hypothesis with information collected by others in the early 1960s. Of course *details* of the land use pattern will have changed but, for the purposes of testing the hypothesis, the published pattern is likely to be as satisfactory as your own field record.

We may analyse the data by comparing the land use pattern with each variable which may have influenced it. We can measure each relationship using a technique such as chi-squared (S.I.G. 3, Chapter 3). The calculations may show, for example, that there is a significant variation of land use with altitude. This suggests that altitude influences the pattern of land use. This concept can be developed only by further study.

Implications

This exercise measures the degree to which two variables are distributed over an area in a similar pattern. The same basic method (with appropriate adaptations in, for example, sampling) can be applied to the relationship between any two variables. For example we can analyse village location and types of surface geology, or rainfall totals and altitude.

Problem 3

How has the distribution of the school or college population changed over the years?

Aim

We might suspect that shifts in the population of the area served by a school have resulted in it being less centrally placed for the current student population. Our aim therefore is to explore the situation by studying the distribution of students in two given years, with an interval of five years between them.

Method

The information is available in the form of the address lists of each of the two years in question. We first take a systematic sample of the same size from each list and then we plot the distribution of these addresses on two maps.

There are a number of ways in which we can use a dot pattern so that a more precise comparison can be made between the two samples (S.I.G. 3, Chapter 6). For example we can calculate both (a) the **mean centre** ('centre of gravity') for each distribution, and (b) the **extent of deviation** (standard distance) from that spatial mean. Thus a picture emerges of the changing patterns, closer examination of which will allow hypotheses concerning the reasons for those changes to be developed.

Implications

In this exercise we do not test a formal hypothesis, but instead study the situation by plotting distributions and using simple descriptive techniques to throw more light on the question. In a similar manner we can test the distribution of any population in relation to one place (perhaps the homes of workers in a certain factory, or the original homes of people who have migrated to an urban area) as a preliminary to our more specific investigation of the hypothesis which arises out of such a study.

Problem 4
How does the stream discharge vary with distance downstream?

Aim
Our aim is to study one stream and to test the hypothesis *that volume of discharge increases in direct proportion to the distance downstream.*

Method
The stream must be long enough for us to take measurements at considerable intervals, yet at no point must it be of such a size that parts of the channel are not easily reached so that measurement of depth becomes difficult. The selection of sample points, at which to measure discharge, presents a number of sampling problems. As we are studying the variations of discharge *along* the stream, and not the (continuous) variations *through time*, we must take the measurements within as short a time-span as possible to minimize possible fluctuations in volume. We should use a systematic sample of points at regular intervals of about 1 km. We must choose, in each case, a convenient straight stretch where the channel is clearly defined as this will help reduce the problems of measuring the stream's discharge.

Having identified a basically systematic sample of places, we can calculate stream discharge at each place from data on the cross-section area of the stream channel and the velocity of flow. For this, we should measure the width of the channel at each place and also the depth of water at a number of points across the channel. These dimensions can be plotted on squared graph paper so that we can draw the cross section of the channel and make an estimate of its area. We can find the surface flow by measuring the average time taken by a number of floats, perhaps 20, to cover a short measured distance at each sample location. To obtain a rough guide to the stream's true velocity, this mean surface velocity should be multiplied by 0·8 (because the water moves fastest at the surface). We can obtain the volume of flow (discharge) at each place by multiplying the calculated values for mean velocity and cross-section area.

Implications
The results of the survey can be plotted on a graph of discharge against distance and, if this produces a straight line, the hypothesis will have been confirmed. If, as is more probable, there are deviations from a straight line, the reasons can be investigated.

There are, of course, other aspects of the variations in channel features which you could examine. For example, is there any notable variation in channel gradient and could this be related to a variable such as surface geology? Following up that idea on a large scale would involve collecting information from geological and topographical maps. Other studies—of pedestrian movements or traffic flow, for example—may be analysed in a similar manner in relation to relevant variables. The variation of flows through time provides another focus of attention and a further range of problems.

Problem 5

Aim

Our aim in this instance is to study the degree of relationship between the character of residential areas and distance from a town centre.

In most towns we can easily observe a tendency for the type of housing to vary with distance from the central area. There are many associated questions worth investigating. Is the rate of change in character a constant one moving outwards from the centre? Does it vary in different sectors of the town? Are there some generalizations about patterns of housing types which are valid for several towns? Using one of these ideas and an index of housing quality, the hypothesis to be tested could be *that there is a direct relationship between price of houses and distance from the town centre.*

Method

For our study we can select several sectors radiating from the town centre and then note details of houses being offered for sale in local newspaper advertisements or estate agents' windows. For each house, we can record distance from the town centre and the price demanded. Of course, some degree of standardization would be necessary concerning the size of houses, perhaps based on the number of bedrooms.

The results for each sector can be analysed in a number of ways. Distance from centre can be plotted against price on a graph to give a general indication of the relationship. We can summarize the trend within a sector by calculating the average price for each distance zone, thus finding both the rate of price change with distance for each zone, and whether the rate of variation of price with distance is constant. This trend provides, for *each sector*, a measure of the extent to which the hypothesis has been confirmed.

Implications

Many subsidiary questions will arise. Is price a satisfactory index of housing character? Do fluctuating prices, inflation, and inconsistent rates of change affect your results? Could the trend have been summarized in a different way? As for the hypothesis itself, it should be emphasized that there was every likelihood that a positive relationship between price and distance would emerge. The interest in interpreting the results comes from asking related questions. Is the trend constant within a sector? Is there similarity between sectors? Where are the major exceptions and how can they be explained?

Variation in house prices is only one type of gradient characteristic of towns' internal patterning. You might be interested in the relationship between distance from town or city centre and another variable, such as amount of open space. In addition to this you can analyse patterns within one town and then attempt to find similar patterns in other towns.

The above examples deal with specifically geographical problems, examining the complex spatial patterns and processes in the environment. On a wider scale, there is a whole range of problems which the geographer can help solve. For example, when it is proposed that local government boundaries should be changed, to which district should a particular area be allocated? The geographer can investigate the spatial aspects of the problem, attempting to answer such questions as 'Where do the loyalties of the area's inhabitants lie?', 'Where do the people work?', 'Where do they shop?'.

Whether the aim is to throw some light on a real-life problem or to test a geographical hypothesis, a properly structured approach, as illustrated in this section, is necessary if something more than the amassing of information is to be achieved. One final point concerning these examples should be stressed. It is important to realize that each emphasizes one facet that stems from a more general area of study. A hypothesis, standing alone, must not be divorced from the examination of the whole complex of processes and characteristics of which it is a part. References here may be made to both Fig. 1.2 and the discussion of systems in geography in S.I.G. 1, Chapter 1.

Chapter 5

Sources

Regularly published statistics that are available in most local libraries were listed in Chapter 3. It is important to realize that there is virtually no limit to the sources, additional to these, from which information for a geographical investigation can be obtained. Indeed, the discovery of previously unsuspected facts during the course of a study—perhaps through a chance meeting with a knowledgeable individual or the unearthing of an obscure document—can often take the problem further than was anticipated. However, as was emphasized on p. 27, it is important to know the most likely sources of relevant information in advance, and to plan the investigation with these in mind.

For any exercise, recording in the field is always one possible way of collecting the necessary information. However, the nature of the topic may be such that field collection methods are inappropriate, or at best can only supply some of the data required. In these circumstances, published sources are the alternative and below are listed, by areas of geographical study, a few of the sources which may be found useful. You may find that a particular investigation does not belong to any of the categories below, or that, if it does, the sources referred to are of little use. It should be noted, therefore, that the purpose of this section is only to suggest the potential value of published information, and with a little ingenuity, you will find that investigation of secondary source material of all kinds can be most productive.

Climatology and meteorology

Most geographers are familiar with the measurement of weather characteristics using instruments of varying degrees of sophistication, mounted in or close to a Stevenson Screen. Records obtained in this way provide an interesting example of the opportunities and pitfalls of collecting statistical information in general. For the records to be acceptable for inclusion in the Meteorological Office's published summaries, the location of the in-

struments must be strictly controlled and the readings should be as continuous and standardized as possible. High standards of recording must be
maintained if the results are to be used for comparison with other stations.
Many schools cannot meet such exacting requirements of location and
continuity. It is therefore important when analysing such data to recognize
and to understand its limitations. A team of inexperienced observers, for
example, will find it difficult to achieve uniformity of Beaufort Scale
judgements, and while the presence of a tall building fairly close to the
Stevenson Screen may be unavoidable, it will have some effect on results.

Even if your recording does not meet official standards, with attention
to the comparability of results through time or between places, detailed
and useful studies of local weather patterns can be undertaken without
purchase of expensive instruments. For example, a team of people can
record the occurrence of mist and fog at certain times in several places.
From this information, such problems as the relationships between the
occurrence of dense fog and altitude, type of environment, or time of day,
can be investigated.

With studies extending over a longer time scale, or over a wider area,
published data summaries can be referred to.*

The *Daily Weather Report* gives a detailed picture of the weather over
Britain and adjacent areas at six-hourly intervals. Maps cover the British
Isles and much of the Northern Hemisphere, while statistical tables give a
breakdown of weather characteristics for 55 British mainland stations and
ocean weather ships.

The *Monthly Weather Report* contains summaries for about 620 stations
in Great Britain and Northern Ireland, together with a review of the
month's weather. An *Annual Summary* of this report is also published.

British Rainfall is an annual publication, including precipitation statistics
from about 6000 stations.

The Meteorological Office also prepares period weather summaries such
as *Averages of Temperature for Great Britain and Northern Ireland,
1931–60.*

Statistics for areas outside the British Isles are difficult to obtain in any
more detail than is given in climatology textbooks.

Geomorphology and soil studies

When the object of an investigation is to study the physical landscape
for its own sake, or to contribute to the understanding of patterns in

*Orders for the reports listed here are dealt with by the Meteorological Office,
Eastern Road, Bracknell, Berks., RG12 2UR.

human geography, there is much scope for measurement techniques. The amount of published data useful for landform studies is small. For example, there are a number of flow gauges on British rivers, and figures for monthly flow are published in the annual *Surface Water Year Book* (HMSO). Details of precipitation and run-off are also given where possible. The network of recording stations is sparse and, while the number of stations is increasing, there are inevitable problems of maintaining continuity, particularly with the siting of flow gauges in the rivers. In spite of this, the data are invaluable for indicating flows over an extended period, and covering large drainage basins. The scale of the data is quite different from, and perhaps complementary to, that of results which can be compiled from field measurement by individuals or small groups.

Published maps are invaluable sources of information on patterns in the physical landscape. Geological Survey maps, solid and drift, on the 1:63 360 scale are in print for many areas of the British Isles. The Soil Survey has prepared maps of a few areas of Britain on the 1:63 360 scale. The familiar 1:63 360—being replaced by the 1:50 000—and 1:25 000 topographical (O.S.) maps, covering the whole of England, Scotland and Wales, are potentially rich sources of geomorphological data. Contour patterns give a general impression of an area's slope characteristics while, where an approximate value for the altitude of a given point is required, the topographical map is clearly the most convenient source. Variations in, for example, valley shape can be explored effectively by the plotting of profiles. The analysis of stream order or drainage density can be approached through the information shown on a 1:25 000 map. Map information has its limitations. For example, slopes cannot be calculated with absolute accuracy from contours with a Vertical Interval as great as 50 feet (15 m); nor can we accurately differentiate stream channels from a mosaic of single blue lines. With these limitations understood however, such relationships as that of stream density to surface geology, valley profile to geomorphological history, or even land use to altitude can be fully examined using map evidence.

Geomorphological field work often involves first-hand identification of salient landscape features from moraines to dry valleys. Not only is such training in recognition an interesting exercise, but there are also notable opportunities for the generation of original data, particularly concerning detailed patterns and movements, neither of which can be derived from map sources. An example of an exercise involving the measurement of stream discharge is given on p. 41. Useful work can also be done in measuring the composition, shape, and size of sedimentary particles, whether they be of alluvial, glacial, or beach material, but particular care should be taken to ensure an attainable objective and a valid sampling method. Gauging pebble sizes, for example, can be a dramatic waste of time if all that is achieved at the end of the day is a long list of figures. Where the aim is to test a particular hypothesis (as on p. 38), however, the painstaking collection of data using quadrat sampling can be justified in terms of the conclusions which may be drawn from the data.

Map information on slope profiles can be supplemented in the field by using simple levelling techniques. A stage further in the analysis of an area's slopes comes with the identification of breaks of slope, separating zones where the slope inclination is relatively uniform. Guidance on morphological mapping techniques is given in articles listed on p. 55.

Where the soils of an area are being examined, many of the variable characteristics, such as depth and acidity, can be readily measured. If a full analysis of the soil profile is needed then a soil pit should be dug, but a soil auger is generally adequate for obtaining samples which can then be tested for such features as texture or moisture content (Wheeler, 1970, Chapter 6). Assuming the use of an appropriate sampling method, conclusions may be drawn concerning the soils of the area. As with other aspects of the environment, the lesson is not that everything in sight should be measured, but that, with a particular aim in mind, many aspects can be studied, often using quite simple collection methods.

Agriculture and rural land use

The plotting of agricultural land use patterns is a well established field work activity. One of a number of sampling methods can be employed where comprehensive coverage of an area is not necessary for the purpose of the investigation. The classification of land use types can be simple or one of some complexity, as in the Second Land Utilisation Survey where 56 categories are recognized. For anyone engaged in a project dealing with land use patterns, the *Land Use Handbook* published in association with this survey is a valuable guide to identification and classification. Information from field observation should be plotted on an outline map of at least scale 1:25 000 (the smallest scale at which field boundaries are shown on O.S. maps). A 1:10 000 map is preferable, as plotting at the smaller scale is likely to be cramped, or even illegible.

The one inch to one mile sheets published in the 1930s provide an interesting documentary source for comparison with the present situation, while the available sheets of the Second L.U.S. (at 1:25 000) perform a similar function, most of the field work for them having been carried out in the early 1960s. Apart from the study of patterns changing through time, there is considerable scope, using topographical and geological map data, for testing hypotheses concerning the degree to which possible influences are spatially related to land use (see p. 39).

For analysing patterns at a different scale, *Annual Agricultural Statistics* (HMSO) gives a breakdown of information for England and Wales by counties, with a separate volume for Scotland.

For global patterns, the *Production Yearbook* is published annually by the Food and Agricultural Organization of the United Nations, with national tables of crops, livestock, size of holdings, etc.

Industry

Distribution patterns of manufacturing and mining enterprises can be recorded from field observation with at least a general indication of the nature of the enterprise. Locations thus recorded can be related to other observable spatial characteristics such as distance from trunk road or distance from city centre. Relationships between industrial location and variables which may have influenced that location pattern can thus be measured. Such a study could concentrate on all manufacturing plants in a small area, or alternatively, widely available secondary sources such as the classified sections of the telephone directory may allow the identification for analysis of all firms whose activities fall into one industrial category.

Where something more is required than a measure of the general attributes of an area, questions put to the firms concerned may be necessary. The existence of, for example, a limestone quarry can be established by observation but questions as to the scale of the enterprise, destination and market for quarried stone, cannot be answered from a distance. Equally, observation may identify a concentration of manufacturing industry along a routeway, but only inquiry will establish the nature of any causal relationship between industry and routeway. Data for individual plants are not normally published. Details such as the number of employees, volume and value of production, sources of raw material, and location of markets for the product can therefore only be obtained from the firms themselves. Such data form a sound base for detailed local analysis of the 'factors' influencing industrial location. It should be appreciated that in any one area the information collected is likely to be incomplete and uneven in quality as firms are understandably reluctant to disclose much of the data in which the geographer is interested.

A *Census of Production* for England and Wales has been taken at intervals, giving national details of production, classified by industrial groups according to the scheme of the Standard Industrial Classification. In the 1963 Census for example, 128 of the 133 volumes and booklets published are concerned with particular industrial groupings.

The *Employment and Productivity Gazette* (HMSO, monthly) gives up-to-date figures of employment, but the *Monthly Digest of Statistics* (HMSO) is probably a more relevant and accessible source for geographical purposes.

Some production and employment information is given in the regional studies, most of which were prepared in the mid-1960s under the Department of Economic Affairs, e.g. *The West Midlands* (HMSO 1965). Though interesting and presented in a digestible form, many of the statistical tables have been superseded by more recent information available elsewhere.

For details of the occupational structure of the employed population in any administrative area, the *Census of Population's Occupation Tables* and *Economic Activity Tables* should be consulted.

The *Digest of Energy Statistics* (HMSO annual) provides data on fuel and power production and consumption.

Information on certain manufacturing industries is available in annual reports and also publications such as *Iron and Steel Industry: annual statistics* prepared by the British Steel Corporation.

These industrial sources are, on the whole, very general in scale, and do not provide the same amount of local detail as some other sources mentioned in this chapter.

Population

Students of population patterns in the United Kingdom have relied to a great extent on the *Census of Population,* published at ten-year intervals since 1801, with the exception of a war-time break in the sequence in 1941. Because local authority areas form the standard enumeration units, changes in boundaries upset the continuity of record, but this is a marginal inconvenience to set against the Census's value to the geographer.

The 1961 Census volumes, for example, range from National Summary Tables giving a broad outline of population throughout the country, to such useful supplementary sources as an Index of Place Names, and National Summaries of Migration. The County Reports, however, are the most likely sources of *local* data. Basic details such as population, area, density, and persons per room, are presented for each ward, the smallest unit distinguished. Other tables, where the data are given for administrative areas, deal fully with housing characteristics, but there are also statistics on such matters as birthplace and nationality. The parallel Censuses of

Scotland and Northern Ireland provide similar, though not identical, information.

The questions asked in gathering material change from one Census to the next, with a general expansion over the years in the volume of data collected. The 1966 Census (a less detailed count taken between 10-yearly censuses) for example, apart from the innovation of taking a sample of the population instead of visiting every household, introduced questions on educational qualifications, place of residence five years previously, and car ownership. New questions in 1971 included those relating to character of work, occupational mobility, and parents' country of birth.

To summarize therefore, the Census of Population not only provides basic information on the location of population, it also indicates the social character of areas through such indices as the density of occupation of dwellings and the socio-economic group to which adult males belong. Furthermore it is a source of data on the migrations of people, whether it be the regular local movements to and from work or the more permanent transfer of people into and out of the United Kingdom.

For information on changes during the intercensal period, the *Annual Estimates of Population* (HMSO) give a useful general picture. Similarly the Government prepares annual reviews of statistics in a wide variety of social fields from education to crime.

National censuses are held at regular intervals in most other countries, but the resulting publications are not readily obtainable outside the country of origin. While the United Nations *Statistical Yearbook* and the U.N.E.S.C.O. *Statistical Yearbook* include some details, the most direct source is the United Nations *Demographic Yearbook*, containing details from the latest national censuses and tables on such matters as the populations of large cities and the patterns of international migration.

Settlement

The borderline between the study of population and the study of settlement patterns is an uncertain one. The geographer frequently gathers data on *population* location or movement primarily in order to throw some light on the character of *settlement*. The emphasis in settlement study however is on the unit which has an observable identity such as a village or a suburban shopping centre. Thus while the Census of Population refers to the area in which that village is situated, the two are not co-extensive and therefore the areal data can only provide background data for the village study. With a large settlement unit such as a conurbation, several Census areas are contained within the boundaries of the unit and so Census data can be of use to some extent in analysing variations within the conurbation.

A great deal of valuable information can be assembled by observing and recording the physical characteristics of the settlement itself. A map of building function or age in a village or in a suburb constitutes a considerable data source, whether one is aiming to study the evolution of the village structure or to analyse the relationships within a shopping centre of shops with similar functions. This is clearly a situation for generating one's own data, while being wary of the problems of identification and classification. Map information concerning the size, function, and location of settlements may then be analysed in various ways.

Published sources are perhaps less valuable in settlement study than in some other areas. While Ordnance Survey maps provide the basic location information, only in the general classification used in the Second Land Utilisation Survey are building functions consistently recorded on published maps. The O.S. maps themselves, even on a large scale, are relatively crude sources of information on building characteristics. While 'Works' and 'Schools' are marked in some cases, the distribution of shops, so significant a feature of any settlement, is not represented; nor of course can the O.S. map be of assistance in studying the three-dimensional character of city centres. However, where patterns of growth are concerned, a sequence of earlier editions of the O.S. map is the most satisfactory means of establishing the nature of settlement growth. A readily accessible source of nineteenth century information is a facsimile of the first edition 1″ Ordance Survey of England and Wales (published by David & Charles Ltd., Newton Abbot, Devon).

When the changing patterns of urban land use are being explored, documentary sources such as directories and rate books provide a comprehensive body of information. Anyone contemplating tapping this source, available in public libraries and council offices, should first consult the article by Davies, Giggs, and Herbert[1], which points out some difficulties likely to be encountered in extracting this information.

The *Census of Distribution* may be included under this heading for, in dealing with retail trade, it contains statistics valuable for analysing the retail aspect of settlements. The full Census of 1961 (the Census of 1966 was a less detailed count) includes tables on the numbers of retail establishments, turnover, etc. Parts 2 to 13 of the 14-volume *Census* deal with the results on an areal basis and so for example, the retail character of any town with a population about 20 000 is fully described.

Questioning a sample of the people resident in a village or those visiting a town for shopping purposes will provide a further source of primary data. The *Census of Distribution* describes the volume and nature of a town's retail trade but the processes at work in sustaining that situation concern the movements of individuals using the shops. In order to establish the retail sphere of influence it is necessary to discover from which area the town's shoppers come. The questionnaire on p. 32 looks from the rural area towards neighbouring towns but, where a particular town is being studied, a set of questions with a similar purpose can be put to a sample of the people shopping in the town (Briggs, 1970[2]). Whichever approach is adopted, there is no published information which could be a substitute for such a questionnaire survey, although certain town planning departments may have the results of recent surveys which may be examined.

Transport and trade

Measurements of traffic flow are a popular form of geographical field work. As discussed on p. 15, the problem lies in relating the population included in the sample (e.g. number of cars passing along a road during one hour) to any larger statistical population. For official purposes, regular road traffic counts are taken either by roadside enumerators or by machines working from the passage of vehicle wheels over a sensor placed in the roadway. The results of these surveys, however, are not normally available to the student.

With passenger traffic by public transport, assuming that the provision of services broadly reflects volume of movement, an analysis of timetables should give a general impression of patterns of movement. Timetables prepared by British Rail and local bus companies are the most readily accessible, but the A.B.C. Guides (published by Thomas Skinner & Co., St. Alphage House, Fore Street, London E.C.2) to coach, rail, airways, air cargo, and shipping give a comprehensive picture of the services throughout the country. With timetables, one is substituting the number of services between A and B for volume of movement which one does not know. Similar timetable information for countries outside the United Kingdom may be available from the London offices of the responsible organization e.g. national railway companies.

Where the route network itself, rather than the movements along it, is being analysed, size, shape, density, connectivity, and relationship to relief can all be satisfactorily measured from an ordinary O.S. map of appropriate scale. The data may then be used to assess the character of the network in terms of, for example, its efficiency, and also, in conjunction with population statistics, to generate hypotheses of traffic flow. Some of the methods of extracting and analysing such data are described by Tidswell and Barker (1971) Chapter 7.[3]

Official government statistics may be obtained from a number of sources published annually by HMSO including:

Passenger Transport in Great Britain;

Highway Statistics;

Annual Report and Accounts of the British Railways Board, or the more specific popular booklet, *Facts and Figures about British Rail;*

Business Monitor: Aviation series which includes four monthly publications, with annual summaries, on such topics as air passengers and airport activity;

Digest of Port Statistics including a breakdown of the character and direction of traffic through British ports;

The Annual Statement of the Trade of the United Kingdom now published in five volumes, contains a full account of external trade by commodities, by countries, by U.K. air and sea ports.

Also, from the British Road Federation, *Basic Road Statistics of Great Britain with a Section on Northern Ireland.*

Regional, national, and local studies

In many of the sources listed above, published data are compiled for the U.K. as a whole or for each of the constituent countries. Detailed information for smaller areas is given in some instances, notably the Census of Population. For other topics, such as agriculture, regional data are available centrally on request but only on payment of a fee. The *Annual Abstract of Greater London Statistics* is one exception to the general rule that it is difficult to obtain data on a variety of aspects of a U.K. sub-region. Where such data are required, the *Abstract of Regional Statistics* can be consulted or national publications searched for information under regional headings.

On the local area scale, only the Censuses of Population and Distribution amongst the published data sources are sufficiently detailed to be of use. For documentary and map evidence of historical trends, County Record Offices or Archives, local museums and libraries are potentially the most fruitful places to search. For recent data on many aspects of the local area, local authority offices can be contacted. Much useful information for geographical study—from the rateable values of each property to proposed patterns of future development—is available to the public. Some authorities are now making special arrangements for students, to allow them to obtain such information without disrupting the working of departments.

Where a study deals with a country or region outside the U.K., reference can be made to statistical sources similar to those published for Britain, as for example the *Statistical Abstract of the United States.* The European Economic Community produces the monthly *General Statistical Bulletin* and the annual *Basic Statistics of the Community.* Copies of data sources for most non-U.K. areas are inevitably difficult to obtain, although much information is included in the publications of the United Nations and its constituent organizations, listed above under the appropriate headings. If one country is being studied and U.K. sources are inadequate, a specific request to that country's London embassy can sometimes prove productive.

References
1. Davies, W.K.D., Giggs, J.A., and Herbert, D.T., 'Directories, Rate Books, and the Commerical Structure of Towns', *Geography*, 53, Part 1 (Jan. 1968).
2. Briggs, K., *Field Work in Urban Geography* (Oliver and Boyd, 1970).
3. Tidswell, W.V., and Barker, S.M., *Quantitative Methods: an Approach to Socio-economic Geography* (University Tutorial Press, 1971).

Further reading for Chapters 3, 4, and 5

Much useful advice on methods of collection is given in textbooks on geographical field work. While general observation and recording methods are fully described, some guidance on the assembling of quantitative data is included in, for example:

Cross, M.F., and Daniel, P.A., *Fieldwork for Geography Classes* (McGraw Hill, 1968).

Wheeler, K.S. (ed.), *Geography in the Field* (Blond, 1970).

Relatively few books deal with the collection and analysis of data on one particular aspect of geography. One such book, with a number of interesting ideas for settlement studies, is:

Briggs, K., *Field Work in Urban Geography* (Oliver and Boyd, 1970).

Some books, while concentrating on methods of *analysing* data, do offer some guidance on ways in which the data can be assembled:

Tidswell, W.V., and Barker, S.M., *Quantitative Methods: an Approach to Socio-economic Geography* (University Tutorial Press, 1971).

Toyne, P., and Newby, P.T., *Techniques in Human Geography* (Macmillan, 1971).

Other books which emphasize analytical techniques may be consulted, both for stimulating ideas, and for the handling of source material:

Everson, J.A., and FitzGerald, B.P., *Settlement Patterns* (Longman, 1969).

Everson, J.A., and FitzGerald, B.P., *Inside the City* (Longman, 1972).

Easily accessible articles which refer to collection methods or the use of sources include:

Davies, W.K.D., Giggs, J.A., and Herbert, D.T., 'Directories, Rate Books, and the Commercial Structure of Towns', *Geography*, 53, pt.1 (Jan. 1968).

Oliver, J.L., 'Directories and their Use in Geographical Inquiry', *Geography*, 49, pt.4 (Nov. 1964).

Keeble, D., 'School Teaching and Urban Geography: Some New Approaches', *Geography*, 54, pt.1 (Jan. 1969).

Everson, J.A., 'Some Aspects of Teaching Geography through Fieldwork', *Geography*, 54, pt.1 (Jan. 1969).

Robertson, I.M.L., 'The National Grid and Social Geography', *Geography*, 55, pt.4 (Nov. 1970).

Derbyshire, E., and Phillips, A.D.M., 'Land Surface Mapping in Westernmost Connemara', *Geography*, 56, pt. 4 (Nov. 1971).

Waters, R.S., 'Morphological Mapping', *Geography*, 43, pt.1 (Jan. 1958).

Clarke, J.I., 'Morphometry from maps', in Dury, G.H. (ed.), *Essays in Geomorphology* (Heinemann, 1966).

Gregory, K.J., and Walling, D.E., 'Field Measurements in the Drainage Basin', *Geography*, 56, pt.4 (Nov. 1971).

Specific techniques of collection and analysis are described in some pamphlets in the *Teaching Geography* series (published by the Geographical Association, 343 Fulwood Road, Sheffield), and the following are particularly useful:

No. 6, Newman, R.J.P., *Field Work Using Questionnaires and Population Data.*

No. 11, Chapallaz, D.P., *et al.*, *Hypothesis Testing in Field Studies.*

No. 14, Morrison, A., *Traffic Study as Quantitative Field Work.*

No. 15, Tidswell, W.V., *An Introduction to the Analysis of Road Networks.*

Appendix A*

Much work in urban areas deals with the business structure of towns, and an efficient classification of shop and business types is necessary. The following classification attempts to split shop and business types into natural groupings, emphasizing their relationship and the processes at work which cause their distinctive patterns.

0 – Convenience stores

(a) Everyday use:

001 General stores
002 General stores and post-office
01 Grocer
021 Newsagent/confectioner/tobacconist
022 as 021, but with a sub-post-office
03 Public house (not 54)

(b) Regular use:

04 Fresh fish
05 Greengrocer/fruiterer
06 Baker (272 not dominant)
07 Butcher
08 Wine store/off licence (not at 03)
09 Chemist

1 – Shoppers' goods stores

10 Clothes–general
101 Clothes–ladies and children
102 Clothes–men
11 Cosmetics/wigs
12 Fancy goods/boutique–general
121 Seaside tourist gifts (rock, cards, etc.)
122 Other tourist-biased gifts and trinkets
13 Furrier

*Source: Everson, J.A., and FitzGerald, B.P., *Inside the City* (Longman, 1972).

14   Jewelry/watches
15   Millinery
16   Shoes–general
161   Shoes–ladies and children
162   Shoes–men
171   Wool/drapery/perhaps some clothes/haberdashery
172   Cloth and fabrics
18   Hardware/domestic appliances (not 39)
19   Radio/TV/electric goods

2 and 3 – Specialist stores

20   Antiques
21   Art dealer
22   Bicycles/prams
23   Books
24   Cameras/photographic materials
25   Chandlery/boat supplies, etc.
26   Florist
27   Foodstores (specialist)
271   Confectioner (only)/sweets
272   Delicatessen (06 not important)
273   Health foods
274   Shell-fish
275   Seaside rock and confectionery
276   Other (specify)
281   Furniture/furnishings/carpets (not 394)
282   Chinaware/glassware/cutlery
29   Leather goods (not 16)
291   Leather goods and some shoe repairs
30   Office furniture
31   Optical goods (not 75, 854)
32   Pets
33   Records/musical instruments, etc.
34   Second-hand/junk/surplus
35   Sports and camping
361   Coin dealer   (both together 36)
362   Stamp dealer
37   Stationery/cards only
371   Tobacconist only
372   Printers

38   Toys/baby goods—general
381   Baby goods only
382   Model shop
391   Builders' merchant
392   Garden supplies
393   Tools
394   Wallpaper/d.i.y.
395   Coal/fuel merchant only

4 – Auto sales

40   Agricultural machinery and servicing
41   Car/motor-bike sales and accessories (no petrol)
42   Car/motor-bike accessories only
43   Garage (workshop and petrol sales)
44   Petrol filling station

45 to 49 spare

5 – Food services

50   Bed and breakfast/board and lodging only
51   Cafe (no meal distinction)
52   Cafe—transport—with significant off-road parking
53   Fried fish and chips
54   Hotel—licensed (Trust House, etc.)
55   Hotel—unlicensed
56   Ice-cream parlour
57   Restaurant (provides meal distinction)
58   Tea rooms (specializes in teas and morning coffee)
59   Wimpey bar

6 – Legal and financial services

60   Bank—normal opening hours
601   Bank—restricted opening (market day, etc.)
61   Betting office
62   Building society office
63   Chartered accountant
64   Estate agent/auctioneer
65   Insurance office
66   Post-office (only)

67 Solicitor/lawyer
68 Trustee savings/mutual savings/loans
69 Spare

7 – General Services

701 Dry cleaners
702 Launderette
711 Electricity showroom
712 Gas show-room
713 Water board show-room
72 Charitable organization (Oxfam, etc.)
731 Hairdresser (gentlemen)
732 Hairdresser (ladies) (together 73)
733 Beauty salon
74 Newspaper offices
75 Optician (not 31, 854)
76 Photographic services (sales not significant)
77 Shoe repairs
78 TV rental (not sales)
79 Travel agent

8 – Educational, religious, and medical facilities, and local government

80 Primary education
801 Nursery/play school
802 Primary school
81 Secondary education
811 Secondary modern school
812 Comprehensive school
813 Grammar school
814 Other secondary school
82 Higher education
821 College of education
822 Technical college
823 University
824 School of motoring
825 Other (specify)
83 Churches, etc.
831 Church—Church of England
832 Church—Methodist

833   Church—Roman Catholic
834   Synagogue
835   Other places of religious worship (not 84)
84   Cathedral
85   Surgery—general
851   Chiropodist
852   Dental
853   General practitioner
854   Ophthalmic
855   Psychiatric
856   Ear specialist/hearing aids
86   Hospital
861   Cottage hospital
862   General hospital
863   Specialist (specify type)
871   Town hall (indicate if it includes 88)
872   Other local government office
88   Library
89   Funeral director

9 – Entertainment

90   Cinema
901   Cinema and significant bingo
902   Cinema—specialist (specify type)
91   Theatre
911   Theatre—specialist (specify)
92   Amusement arcade or park
93   Billiard/snooker hall
94   Bingo (only)
95   Bowling alley
96   Club—not included elsewhere (specify)
97   Skating rink
98   Sports ground
99   Swimming pool

X—Department and chain stores, etc.

X0   Boots/Timothy Whites
X1   Co-op department store
X2   Marks and Spencer

X3   Sainsbury/David Greig
X4   W. H. Smith
X5   F. W. Woolworth
X6   Supermarket (e.g. Fine Fare, etc.)
X7   Other department store (specify)
X8
X9   spare (use to suit local circumstances)

Also

A   Allotments/private small holdings
B   Builder's yard/contractor
F   Factory
Of   Offices (not included elsewhere)
N   Nursery (plants)
P   Car park
Pm   Car park—multi-storey
T   Timber merchant's yard
V   Vacant
W   Warehouse

E — Extra categories (not included above)

E1   (fill in as appropriate)
E2
E3

Appendix B*

Methods of data collection for: 1. Measuring pedestrian flow
                                          2. Pedestrian density

1. A static pedestrian count may be undertaken in order to illustrate the general pattern of pedestrian movement. By measuring flows into and out of certain major road intersections it should be possible to locate within the town the intersections which enjoy maximum pedestrian accessibility. The static pedestrian count should be taken at previously

Count sections are denoted by pecked
lines between arrows thus: ←– – b – – →

Count points are denoted
by figures thus: —6—

*Sketch map showing suitable
positions for count points
and sections on a hypothetical
road network*

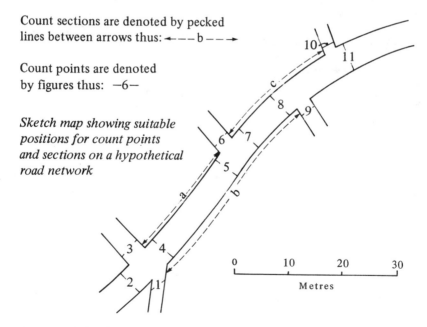

*Source: adapted from Chapallaz, D.P. et al., Hypothesis Testing in Field Studies, Teaching Geography Series No.11 (Geographical Association, 1970).

Location	Time	Moving into intersection	Moving out of intersection
Count point no: _ _ _			
	Total:		

Static pedestrian count recording sheet

Location	Length	Time	Number of Pedestrians	Pedestrian density
Count section no: _ _ _				
		Average:		

These counts should be averaged rather than totalled

Moving pedestrian count recording sheet

determined points and at specific times. The times chosen should avoid all periods of unusual activity, e.g. rush hours, unless this is to be specifically investigated. The results may be recorded as on the record sheets illustrated above. The count should last for a set period of time (e.g. five minutes as a minimum) during which the total number of pedestrians passing the observer in each direction on both sides of the road should be noted. Distinction must be made between pedestrians moving *into* the intersection close to the count point and those moving *out* of it.

2. 'Pedestrian density' is the number of pedestrians per unit length of pavement. This could be taken to be a standard unit of 10m.

Pedestrian density can be measured by means of a moving pedestrian count; the observer should walk at a steady pace along the length of a count section noting the total number of pedestrians he meets coming in the opposite direction together with those he passes who are walking more slowly than he is in the same direction. Persons looking into shop windows should also be counted provided that they are on the pavement itself and not on the shop premises. Only pedestrians of school age and over should be counted. This total should be recorded in the appropriate place. The count sections are normally continuous strips of pavement (between about 20 and 100 metres in length) which have no interruptions caused by car parks and vacant buildings, or intersections with other streets. Each count section should contain some homogeneity of character in land use and the sections should be planned beforehand on Ordnance Survey 1:1250 ('50 inch') base map, parts of which might be re-drawn and then duplicated for the observers' use.

Contents of Science in Geography, books 1, 3, and 4

S.I.G. 3   Data description and presentation

Peter Davis

Contents

S.I.G. 4   Data use and interpretation

Patrick McCullagh